PARTNERS
WITH THE POOR

*An Emerging Approach
to Relief and Development*

JERRY AAKER

Friendship Press • New York

Copyright © 1993 by Friendship Press

Editorial Offices:
475 Riverside Drive, New York, NY 10115

Distribution Offices:
P.O. Box 37844, Cincinnati, OH 45222-0844

Manufactured in the United States of America

Library of Congress Cataloging-in-Publication Data

Aaker, Jerry.
    Partners with the poor : an emerging approach to relief and
development / Jerry Aaker.
        p.   cm.
    Includes bibliographical references and index.
    ISBN 0-377-00252-6
    1. Church work with the poor—Developing countries. 2. Economic
development—Religious aspects—Christianity. 3. Church and state—
Developing countries. 4. Lutheran World Relief—History.
I. Title.
BV639.P6A235 1993
261.8'325'091724—dc20   92-35591
                                                              CIP

PARTNERS
WITH THE POOR

Contents

Foreword

This book is a report "from the front." Jerry Aaker writes of his experiences where the human fight for survival is most intense and precarious. Summarizing more than twenty-five years of remarkable service by him and his wife, he writes of a will to "endure in the face of pessimism." Their motivation is clearly their Christian faith. As a personal odyssey, the account provides an encouraging example and stimulus for any who seek to live out a commitment to helping others to a better life.

The personal reflections awakened memories of the even longer odyssey of American organizations engaged in overseas aid and development since World War II. When the United States government moved away from retaliation against wartime enemies to a plan of reconstruction for both friend and foe, volunteer organizations stood ready to help. Churches organized agencies primarily concerned for fellow Christians in the lands of the immigrant origins of their members.

The relief work extended to overseas mission fields of the churches, a major shift in emphasis when Europe no longer needed assistance. America's place as a global power, no longer dominated by isolationism, became clearer in terms of "One World." The movement to economic development for "underdeveloped" countries did not automatically attract the support of all church leaders. This activity of the churches benefited persons of a variety of religions. In many places Christian witness is restricted to unselfish service without explicit proclamation of the Gospel. The sense of kinship was diminished, and as a result the altruism of the Good Samaritan had to be developed.

The decision to participate in overseas development work had been made before I was first elected to the board of directors of Lutheran World Relief, but the questions continued to be discussed among the supporting church constituency. As time moved on, new debates occurred about the effectiveness of economic development projects. These issues found a place in the agendas of many board meetings.

Jerry Aaker deals with these topics in a most helpful way. Working for three different church-sponsored agencies, he does not settle for theorizing about abstractions. He is the kind of field staff person whom employing agencies seek and respect. His social-service training and experience help when working with people in desperate situations. His skills make him capable of moving beyond charity and the distribution of relief supplies.

He also learned from experience. With an ability to perceive the effects on people of the work he was doing, he could grasp new possibilities. In company with other workers, he became sensitive to the need for human development that was more than economic improvement. He saw how people could exert initiative and participate in community development and how a sponsoring agency rejecting paternalistic dependency can adopt methods of accompaniment and partnership.

Fortunately for the reader, Jerry Aaker articulates well his reflections on the many issues he has had to deal with. The scope is comprehensive. Although these matters had been discussed at board meetings and conferences, they come alive when the author describes them in terms of his own experience and growth. I am grateful that such understanding is now available to the many who have supported efforts to overcome hunger, deprivation, and oppression.

Committed as he is to fostering greater justice through human development, Jerry Aaker does not present any proposal as an uncritical promoter. He insists on portraying both the merits and demerits of each approach to human betterment. Still, his conviction is clear that Christians from different parts of the world can benefit from combining their distinctive gifts to learn from each other and work for a common purpose. He shows how nongovernmental, private, voluntary organizations can play a crucial role in relating to people who seek a new future.

Robert J. Marshall
President, Lutheran World Relief

Acknowledgments

Many of the ideas presented in this book have been learned from colleagues and friends with whom I worked in programs of relief and development for many years. Some of these colleagues are from the "South," mostly Latin Americans, and some from the many "Northern" organizations and programs with which I have had the privilege to serve.

More importantly, I have learned many lessons from people living in poor communities in Latin America, Asia, and Africa. The poor have much to teach us about community, care for the earth, and simple living. Through interaction with them I have often been renewed in spirit and challenged to persevere in the face of the logic of pessimism.

A few of the colleagues and friends who helped shape my thinking and challenged me through the example of their lives to stick with it over the years are: Peter and Paula Limburg, Neal and Marta Brenden, Pat and Earl Martin, Abner and Martha Batalden, Helen and Gene Braun, Gustavo Parajón, Gilberto Aguirre, Octavio Cortez, Mario Padrón, Bernie Confer, J. Robert Busche, Larry Minear, Hans Hoyer, Jim DeVries, Gorden Hatcher, and Walter Blake.

Several colleagues merit special mention. Pedro Veliz of Lutheran World Relief's Andean Regional Office has made valuable contributions to the evolution of the agency's accompaniment approach to development assistance. In many ways, Pedro is the embodiment of LWR's walking with the poor in the Andean region.

Norman Barth, executive director of Lutheran World Relief, who felt it was important to document some of what we have learned about relief and development, gave me much support and encouragement to do so. Thanks to Kathryn

Wolford and Charles Lutz for their insights and critique of early drafts, and Ann Beretta for challenging me to clarify concepts and for her valuable help with editing. A special word of thanks goes to Bill Gentz for his patient encouragement and skill as editor and advisor. He helped to bring it all together.

None of these people bears responsibility for the opinions or for any errors that this book may contain. Though Lutheran World Relief is sponsoring this volume, the opinions written here are not necessarily those of LWR. The views expressed are solely mine.

Finally, thanks to my wife, Judy, who was with me through the years and made valuable contributions to accompanying the poor in her own way. Our sojourn brought us to many places where we faced both discouragements and challenges, highs and lows, joys and loneliness. I thank her for that accompaniment.

Acronyms

ADFF Andean Development Facilitation Fund

ARO Andean Regional Office (of Lutheran World Relief)

CARE major U.S. nongovernmental organization for relief and development

CEPAD Council of Churches (of Nicaragua); originally Comité Evangélico para Ayuda al Desarrollo, the Evangelical Committee for Aid to Development.

CRS Catholic Relief Services

CWS Church World Service

HPI Heifer Project International

LCA Lutheran Church in America

LWR Lutheran World Relief

MCC Mennonite Central Committee

NGO Nongovernmental Organization

USAID United States Agency for International Development

VNCS Vietnam Christian Service

PARTNERS
WITH THE POOR

Introduction

"REMEMBER THE POOR"

Fathers Bill Woods, Juan Alonso, Carlos Gálvez, Stan Rother, and Walter Voordeckers all had something in common. They were priests serving the people of Guatemala, and they all lost their lives in that service during the worst of the violence and repression that afflicted that country during the 1980s.[1] It was their call to work with the poor in that land of eternal spring. This beautiful country with its colorful culture, a mixture of Mayan and Spanish influences, is also a place of extreme poverty and malnutrition. Half the population lives on incomes of $80 a year or less, especially the native Indian groups. These descendants of the great Mayan civilization are some of the most marginated and forgotten people in the hemisphere.

During the great furor about Central America in the 1980s, the outside world focused most of its attention on Nicaragua and El Salvador. Meanwhile the Guatemalan people were experiencing tremendous violence and some of the worst human rights abuses in the world in the midst of grinding poverty, yet little attention was paid to them.

Tourists, the press, and politicians showed little interest in Guatemala, but churches and other private relief and development agencies continued to support the poor where and when they could in out-of-the-way places in that country. One of the main purposes was simply to be there and do what could be done to empower those who were suffering the worst effects of poverty and repression. Those in

3

power often see this kind of activity as a threat, and death squads threatened, tortured, and killed many of the leaders of groups that sought to organize the poor. Some of the priests listed above lost their lives because they elected to stay with the people they served and loved even in the face of death threats. They witnessed to their faith by accompanying the poor.

I traveled to Guatemala many times during the height of the repression as a program director of Heifer Project International. Each time I posed these questions to the Guatemalans who were carrying out projects to help the poor: "Is it really possible to continue to work under these conditions? Would it be better if we as outside churches and agencies were not involved here right now? Isn't it putting you in jeopardy to be running these aid and development projects?" Each time the answer came back, "Now more than ever we need your support. We need to stay organized in some way. We must continue."

There are many "Guatemalas" in the world where programs of relief and development are being carried out far from the spotlight of world attention. In fact, the world's attention span is not very long. When agencies like Heifer Project, Lutheran World Relief, or Church World Service, the organizations with which I have been involved for over twenty-five years, enter into programs of poverty alleviation and development, it takes a concerted effort to stick with it over the long haul. These agencies understand the meaning of being partners with the poor in both emergencies and in long-term programs of assistance.

"Compassion fatigue" is a term that is used by fund raisers to explain why the public can no longer be convinced to contribute to seemingly intractable and endless needs. Whether we are confronted by the ongoing crisis of famine in sub-Sahara Africa or a long-term development program in a Central American country, carry-through and perseverance are crucial. Commitment and continuity are often the key elements to effectiveness in promoting human development.

In his Epistle to the Galatians, St. Paul records an account of a meeting with leaders and co-workers of the young churches to discuss their mission to the gentiles. They probably discussed doctrine, plans, and strategies. There were still many things unresolved at the conclusion of their meeting, but they agreed on one thing: "All they asked was that we should continue to remember the poor, the very thing I was eager to do" (Gal. 2:10).

There are many theories and strategies for service to the poor, but it is not easy for us as people from comparatively rich churches in rich countries to "continue to remember the poor." We get frustrated because of the slowness of the process of real change. We doubt that any real progress is being made, and so we tend to put the problem out of mind until we feel good about doing something.

This book describes the efforts of church-related relief and development agencies to accompany and "help" the poor, a mandate to which both individual Christians and specialized agencies are called. The book is written for people who are interested in knowing how assistance programs have been and are being carried out in low-income countries by churches and nongovernment organizations.

Our purpose is to communicate to people who are motivated to work for real and lasting change in a very unjust and hungry world. We will discuss some of the pitfalls as well as the strengths of various approaches that have commonly been used in assistance programs in the past several decades. The book is written for those who believe that it is important to persist and "continue to remember the poor." It is an attempt to think about the proper response of people of conscience to the challenges of poverty and injustice in this decade and beyond. My hope is that it will help us all as we think collectively about the great challenges ahead of us.

OVERVIEW

I write from experience. Part I of this book describes some personal attempts at working with poor communities in the

Two-Thirds World, some successfully and some ending in relative failure. The terms "Two-Thirds World" and "One-Third World" are used to designate the division between the less developed and economically developed countries. With the crumbling of much of the "Second World" — (the socialist bloc) — the term "Third World" seems to have less meaning. Another commonly used term is "low-income countries." In this book I also use the terms "North" and "South" as a contrast between rich and low-income countries.

Reflecting on efforts to do relief and development, we examine twenty-five years of work in a career that has touched most aspects of what private relief and development agencies do. What should be done in programs of disaster response, community development, institution building, accompaniment of local organizations, and aid administration? We begin in war-torn Vietnam, then move to disaster responses in Peru and Nicaragua, and development programs in these and other Latin American countries. It has been my good fortune during these years to have been associated with some of the best organizations the church has established: Lutheran World Relief, Heifer Project International, and Church World Service.

This book is an account of part of my personal and professional sojourn through this labyrinth that is commonly called the relief and development field. I call it a wandering because the journey has been more of an exploration and response to needs and calls for help than a career of predefined goals.

Part II presents a theoretical framework from which to approach the complicated and difficult challenges of work with the world's poor communities. In reviewing four different models of "human development," I draw upon some of the writings of a Brazilian with much first-hand experience, Frances O'Gorman. These approaches are (1) assistance, or humanitarian aid, (2) teaching, or the education approach, (3) participatory development projects, and (4) transformation. In this section I will attempt to summarize these four models, taking some of the basic concepts from O'Gorman and adding other examples and ideas from my own experiences in Latin America and elsewhere. The paraphrasing and translations from Spanish are mine. A final chapter in this section deals with some questions that are often asked by people in the churches about relief and development programs.

Part III is an effort to systematize some experiences in the Andean region of South America as carried out by Lutheran World Relief, with special attention to Peru. It is there that considerable energy has been concentrated on an approach that we call "accompaniment." I first take a look at the Latin American context and some of the factors that gave rise to the idea of accompaniment. Secondly, my Peruvian colleague and friend Pedro Veliz put together much of the description of the work of Lutheran World Relief's Andean Regional Office. For almost a decade Pedro has creatively and tirelessly worked at the task of accompanying LWR partners in the Andean region. This case study is followed by a description of some of the principles as well as specific tools of accompaniment, the "how to do it" part of this study.

Throughout the book questions keep occurring. What role do people of conscience and faith have in this great challenge of walking with the poor in a relationship that ensures dignity for both sides of a partnership? What does it take to function in a helpful relationship? What models of promoting human betterment really work? What are our basic attitudes toward the poor?

Finally, the last chapter presents a challenge for the future. I take a look at some of the tasks that people of faith need to address in a world of increasing inequity, overpopulation and violence. Where do individuals and institutions fit into this mesh of "doing good"? How do lay people and church leaders become involved in accompanying the poor? The need is great for a shared and common vision within our churches and institutions. Perseverance is required if we are to act on that vision and continue day by day to "remember the poor."

Part I

WANDERINGS THROUGH THE HELPING PROFESSION

Development is a very young profession. Some of its precedents and historical roots are found in community development work done in colonial Africa and in church mission efforts in agriculture and health, often on compounds and in institutions. After World War II, reconstruction and technical assistance programs sponsored by governments grew into a major effort of the economically developed countries.

In the 1960s there was a fervor among Americans to "go overseas" and help people in poor countries pull themselves out of their underdeveloped condition. Thousands of volunteers went into the Peace Corps, and churches had relatively large contingents of missionaries overseas. Official development assistance programs, like the United States Agency for International Development (USAID), had built up a large presence in many countries.[1] Organizations that had been founded as relief agencies in the post-war period were turning to the ideas of self-help and community development. Nevertheless, many of them still had (and have) the relief or service connotation in their names: Lutheran World *Relief* (LWR), Church World *Service* (CWS), Catholic *Relief* Services (CRS).

Many respected nongovernmental organizations (NGOs) that work in development today were first set up to help victims of World War II. The three organizations with which I have spent most of my career — LWR, CWS, and Heifer Project International (HPI) — all share this history. HPI, for example, was founded by Dan West, an Indiana farmer who went to Spain during the Spanish civil war to do relief work. When he saw the futility of handing out milk to hungry children who came back day after day for more, he conceived the idea of "rather than a cup of milk, give a family a cow."[2] After World War II, HPI sent thousands of dairy cattle to families in the devastated countries of Europe. The ingenious principle of "passing on the gift" (i.e., a recipient family gives an offspring animal to a second family) contained early seeds for the idea of self-help rather than relief as a premise of helping people affected by disaster or poverty.

Many years later Lucy West Rupel, the widow of Dan West, reflected, "Hundreds in line would come past the table where they were doling out powdered milk. Dan had to say, 'What's the use?' So he started just dreaming and, really, it was very simple — not a cup, but a cow."

My career in development has somewhat coincided with the growth of the development industry and has been influenced by insights from collective as well as personal experience. Over the years many mistakes have been made by both governmental and private organizations and individuals, including myself, sometimes at high cost. In this kind of work we need both the dreamers and the doers, and I think there is a bit of both in my experience. I believe that learning has taken place during these years, and we are in a better position today to face the challenges of this decade and the twenty-first century because of lessons from the past. Better documentation and research are becoming available to development professionals, and sounder theories are being expounded.

Nevertheless, some research has raised questions as to whether nongovernmental organizations are as effective as they are purported to be at achieving what is claimed to be their special area of competence. Based on a study of NGO work in Colombia, Brian H. Smith concludes that, while local NGOs do effective work in helping the poorest sectors of the population, these efforts are largely supported by outside resources and evidence of their sustainability is inconclusive. Though they demonstrate considerable innovation, there is little replication of their strategies or influence on public policy within the country.[3]

Obviously, we need to continue to do research and evaluations to see if this is true in the cases of programs we support. A hard-nosed look at what we are achieving is required by those working as professionals in this field. The donors who support relief and development programs deserve accountability.

David C. Korten, one of the most prolific researchers in the development field today, has described three generations of voluntary development action.[4] His contention is that private agencies, like LWR and HPI, have or are going through three distinct stages. The first is that of relief and welfare — the provision of material assistance. The second is self-help community development on a project-by-project basis. The third moves into looking for the accumulative effect of sustainable development strategies and trying to influence policy on a micro-level. Indeed, a fourth generation is suggested, that of mobilizing people's movements with a global change perspective, one that very few, if any, development NGOs have moved into to date.[5]

It takes tremendous concentration and intentional effort to move into the third generation, given the constant pull to respond to needs out of first- and second-generation approaches. Many of us have been working toward third-generation strategies over the last few years, even as numerous agencies still put major resources into relief efforts and individual development projects.

The "accompaniment" approach, which Lutheran World Relief has espoused as a methodology of work in the Andean region of South America, is an attempt at a third-generation philosophy. Ups and downs can be expected on this path by serious NGOs in their attempt to be relevant and true to their own mission.

I have personally gone down the road of varying models through the years. Not surprisingly, it is not a clear and systematic movement from one generation to the next, but a weaving back and forth along several tracks at the same time. It is little wonder that one feels the need to get off the train from time to time to take a look at where we have been and where we are going.

Chapter One

VIETNAM
Starting on the Cutting Edge

In 1966 my wife, Judy, and I were asked to consider going to Vietnam to take part in a major effort by several
church-related relief agencies in that war-ravaged country.
Ove Nielsen of Lutheran World Relief called us at our home
in Minnesota one cold and snowy morning in January to ask
if we would be willing to be a part of LWR's response to
the massive human needs being created by the war in Vietnam. Like most Americans, we were following the news of
the deepening quagmire that our country was getting into in
that part of the world. It was obvious that the effect of this
war was particularly devastating for the civilian population
in Vietnam.

In 1965 three agencies, Mennonite Central Committee,
Church World Service, and Lutheran World Relief, had
joined together to form Vietnam Christian Service (VNCS).
For the next ten years this program channeled millions of
dollars of aid, along with several hundred expatriate personnel, to Vietnam. Many of the people who served in
this program were draft-age Mennonite men who took the
conscientious objector option to go to Vietnam to work
as volunteers in a humanitarian program with the civilian
population.

VNCS was a major undertaking by the U.S. churches to
insert both a witness for peace as well as a relief and service
program into that tragic war which brought such trauma
and destruction to both Vietnam and the U.S. Unfortunately,

13

the overall meaning and learnings from this experience have
not yet been fully documented by those who participated in
this effort.[1]

We accepted the challenge with much apprehension. In
July of 1966 we arrived in Saigon to begin a two-year term
of service, Judy as a nurse and I as a social worker.

LEARNING FROM SCRATCH

Many of us who served in VNCS were relatively young professionals in the social work, medical, clergy, management,
and agricultural fields. Others were generalists with no specific professional training, but with a high motivation to
serve. We all went with a strong desire to "make a contribution" and a tangible difference in the lives of those affected
by the war, but with virtually no training for that task. We
were notably inexperienced and unprepared for what we
encountered in that convoluted human drama that was Vietnam in the 1960s and 1970s. Though we had been trained
in the principles and skills of the helping professions in our
home countries (most of us were from Canada and the U.S.),
we knew very little of "development" as a profession or field
of study. Nor did we know much about "relief work." Few
of us had cross-cultural training, and the level of language
proficiency that most of us were able to attain on short two-
or three-year terms was another limiting factor. Once on the
field we had little choice but to plunge in, improvise, and
learn how to do our jobs as we went along. Obviously, there
are dangers and pitfalls along this route.

BEING A PRESENCE

We began to learn that charity can run in shallow as well
as deep streams. Charity acted out as paternalism can be
degrading and promote inequality. A deeper understanding
of charity leads to a commitment to others as equals, even

when the other is in a weak or underprivileged situation. It can even lead to giving up one's life for a cause deeply believed in.

As time went on those who were serving with VNCS seemed to choose one of two general categories of thinking about our purpose for being there. A substantial contingent of our colleagues felt strongly about doing something very concrete to help the suffering civilian population. We were there to "serve in the name of Christ." Another group felt that simply being "a presence" in the midst of great human suffering was enough to justify the effort, risk, and cost. In fact, for those who held this position, simply being there was a statement of witness and solidarity and was about all we could expect to do. At that time in my career I suppose I fell into the first group of those who wanted to see the results of our efforts to alleviate the suffering of a war-ravaged people.

The idea of "being with" follows the biblical mandate and challenge of offering the cup of cold water to the sufferer, the sick, and the oppressed. This is a fundamental human response of charity motivated by love. In fact, this was the motivation out of which our sending agencies and many other agencies founded in the post–World War II period have their roots and reason for being.

Those who espouse the concept of presence think that people are the most important resource. Organizations like the Mennonite Central Committee and the Church of the Brethren, who pioneered volunteer programs as an outlet for service and an alternative to military service, specialize in placing volunteers in areas of need in many parts of the world. In these programs it is often argued that the benefits flow in two directions. The home churches and sending country greatly benefit from the learning and consciousness raising that happens when volunteers are engaged with poor communities. Volunteers bring back to their own society a heightened understanding of the problems of injustice and interdependence in today's world.

WITNESS FOR PEACE

The idea of "witness for peace" was a strong motivation on the part of many of our colleagues. The majority of us, in fact, were opposed to the U.S. involvement in the Vietnam War and wanted to make a commitment to stand alongside those who were the innocent victims of war and violence, even in the face of real personal danger. This is not new in the Christian tradition, especially among the denominations known as the "peace churches," such as the Mennonites and the Church of the Brethren.

The laying down of one's life for this cause occurred in several instances to colleagues who served with Vietnam Christian Service. One of them was Ted Studabaker, a young man who served in the same village, lived in the same house, and worked in the same position as I had during our first year in Vietnam. In a major attack by North Vietnamese regulars and local Vietcong, the village of Dilinh was over-run and Ted was cut down by gunfire as he was moving from the house to a bunker outside.

In later years we were to relive that tragedy many times in our minds, imagining what we would have done had we been in that house the night of the attack on our village. What goes through one's mind in the last moments and seconds of life when actually "laying down your life" for something you believe in?

At the time of the Chinese New Year, known as Tet, which in 1968 fell in early February, the whole country exploded in an attempt by the Vietcong to end the war with a final massive offensive. In a letter I tried to put into words some of the tensions and feelings we were experiencing:

All through the week we live in tension. Then into the second week — wondering how many more days it will last. The rumors run wild, and each time we gather as a group and talk too long we come away having frightened each other more than gaining the hoped-for comfort.

We have good intentions — we came here to help, but now our hands are tied, it seems. We can do so little. We feel frustrated and discouraged. We fear the worst for fellow workers in Hue, but still no report as day after day passes. Now with each new cable I read Sam's face [Sam Hope, our director of personnel] before I read the text — a sigh of relief, as another colleague has reported in safe.

We joke together, but our talk belies inner anxiety. No one dares verbalize how profoundly he or she wishes they were not here. It would be chicken to leave — after all, we are committed Christians. They tell us we are the church at work and a Christian presence among the suffering here. How pathetic, we say to ourselves, as we realize how impotent we are, how weak we are compared to the massiveness of this conflict. How the forces of destruction seem to overpower the forces of peace and life.

I saw a thousand homes that had been destroyed in a day. I listened to the stories of fellow workers who had lived through terror, where women and children were shot in the back of the head and bombs fell from planes screaming above at 400 miles an hour. I saw the faces of Vietnamese as night draws near, and they wondered if they would see the morning. I heard the proclamations of a "glorious victory" — 25,000 "enemy" killed in a week. Mind boggling! Are we supposed to be proud? I saw refugees and watched the statistics climb, 200,000 uprooted from their homes in Saigon. When the numbers go so high my confused mind fails to comprehend. I read the letters from worried parents, and choke up as I realize how they are worrying. I feel the house shake and the windows rattle as bombs fall and explode.

I have no conclusions, just thoughts and feelings. But after a while we stop to think of the presence of God. If we really believe that all things work together for good for those who love God, then

we must try to decipher some sense from this confusion.

Now to pick up the pieces we must stretch our creativity to the utmost. There is a job to be done and we
start slowly, with some false starts and frustrations as
we go along. Days pass in which we are unable to do
anything because of the problem of security. But little
deeds done may mean a lot in this place now. Some of
our people start hauling firewood to refugee centers,
bringing water to bombed-out areas, and bread to the
neediest. We start to lay bigger plans for the Saigon
area, at the same time as we have to make decisions to
pull out of some of our up-country projects.

The program has taken a turn in one after another
of our projects, and we must report that in many ways
we can do much less now, even though we feel the
urge to do more and the financial backing pours in
from around the world.

We have now sent some of the wives and children
away and soon several more will leave. Three weeks
after the beginning of this new phase of the war we
are re-evaluating. We are thankful that all our people
are safe and well. We are saddened by the death of six
missionaries, two of whom were good friends of ours.
We are saddened by the destruction of large parts of
towns, especially the beautiful city of Hue.

Saigon, March 1968

Two decades later, in the 1980s, a strong witness for peace
movement was at work in Central America, especially in the
strife-torn countries of Nicaragua, El Salvador, and Guatemala. Some of the most heroic acting out of the meaning of
accompaniment — literally standing with the poor and oppressed in the face of danger — was seen in those countries.
In fact, in numerous cases expatriate volunteers assumed
positions of shielding those who were in vulnerable and
dangerous situations.

One such case is that of the tiny but courageous Lutheran Church in El Salvador, whose work with refugees and the poor has put church leaders and field personnel of social ministry programs in continuous danger. In these circumstances it has been conjectured that a foreign presence provides protection, because of raised international visibility. In some cases it is certainly true that such a presence has served this purpose, because of the increased complexity involved for the perpetrators when a foreigner is detained, tortured, or killed.

Unfortunately, this supposition has not always been accurate, as manifested in the many cases of martyrdom that have occurred in those Central American countries for over a decade. The words of Father César Jerez, the Jesuit provincial for Central America in 1977, "We will stay until we fulfill our duty or are liquidated," were chillingly prophetic, given the brutal murder of six Jesuit priests in San Salvador more then a decade later.

INTERPRETING THE EXPERIENCE

The Vietnam War helped us personally and helped the church at large to become aware of the political implications of service. Earl Martin, a Mennonite volunteer, wrote this reflection ten years after the termination of the war:

> The people of God learned in Vietnam that to serve "apolitically" calls for service which in fact carries tremendous political impact.... In a political or military conflict, both antagonists will attempt to appropriate the impact of Christian service for their own ends. When we gave food and support to displaced farmers in the refugee camps, we could be seen as giving support to the dependents of the revolutionary guerrillas. Or, seen from another light, we might have been helping to "win hearts and minds" to the American war effort.... In an arena of intense conflict, all human activity becomes politicized. The challenge for the church

is to focus on principles of the gospel and be divinely oblivious of the attempts by one side or the other to politicize our service.[2]

In Vietnam we talked a lot about being neutral, about trying to demonstrate through our actions and lives that we wanted to give aid impartially, based on the criteria of need. Nevertheless, there were few of us who personally knew if the Vietnamese we were relating to and helping were Vietcong sympathizers. We assumed that many were. We did not ask, and the information, of course, was not volunteered.

Among the most frequent questions asked of us when we later made presentations in churches in the United States about our Vietnam experiences were: "What did the Vietnamese people really think about Americans? Did they appreciate your attempts to help them?" It seems to me that these questions reflect a mindset that is quite natural and probably very American. We *want* to be liked and appreciated for our good intentions of helping the needy and for trying to make things right in an unjust world. However, my answer to both questions had to be, "I really don't know; it is difficult to generalize about such things."

I can now reflect on the question of appreciation from a much broader experience in other countries and participation in many relief programs. It seems to me that the level of people's response to help is directly related to the degree they have been deprived and dehumanized. On the one hand I have seen tremendous pride, appreciation, and feelings of dignity and responsiveness in people who participate in programs in which they are given the chance to help themselves and others through communal sharing. In contrast to that, I have images of humiliated refugees who had been bombed out of home and community, existing in relocation camps on the coast of Vietnam, completely dependent on feeding programs from benevolent outsiders. How would anyone feel about that?

Our work was interpreted to the church constituency through several articles in church publications during the time we were in Vietnam. One of these put it this way: "Lutherans and other personnel with Vietnam Christian Service are bringing Christian concern, love and compassion as well as help and skills to war-torn Vietnam. . . . In an atmosphere of pain and suffering, of moral breakdowns inevitable in time of war, and frequently of hopelessness, they work to rebuild bodies, persons, families and communities."[3] A big order, indeed!

LEAVING SOMETHING BEHIND

In Vietnam we talked a good deal about leaving something lasting behind. In many cases we worked alongside Vietnamese counterparts and with Vietnamese institutions, such as hospitals and rehabilitation centers, but most of our work consisted of the "do-it-ourselves" variety of aid. We ran refugee feeding programs, hospitals, and day-care centers, and initiated public health, craft marketing, and small agricultural projects. We expatriates, "Westerners" as we called ourselves, tried to work directly with the people in rural communities, refugee camps, and urban slums. Though we hired and worked with local staff, "Nationals" as we called them, we were in charge and ran the programs. Though there were attempts at community development, perhaps the best term to describe the programs in which we were involved would be "provision of services," modeled primarily on the social work and medical professions.

In retrospect, perhaps the primary thing of lasting value was the training provided for a number of Vietnamese staff of VNCS, such as social workers, nurses, and administrators. The irony was that this was not something that was necessarily "left behind." Many of those trained people fled to the U.S. after the chaotic close of the war and change of government in 1975.

What was left inside of us who participated in VNCS

was a lasting impression of the smallness of our contribution in the face of the massive political forces that perpetrate war. Nevertheless, we felt that the only appropriate response was to do something, even if that was simply to be present.

Chapter Two

PERU

Learning at the Grassroots

In 1969, after the baptism by fire into international relief and service in Vietnam, we were asked by the Lutheran Church in America (LCA) to go to Peru for three years. At that time the LCA was supporting mission work in the *barriadas* of Lima, the massive urban slums that were springing up on the desert around the capital city. The mission wanted to initiate a social outreach program alongside the evangelism and church planting the missionaries were doing with the urban poor.

THE CHALLENGE OF LIMA

After some months of Spanish language studies and cultural orientation in Mexico, we arrived in Peru in May 1970, ready to go to work, or at least to find out what the work was supposed to be. The job description and mandate for my work went something like this: study the social problems in the poor slums of Lima and make recommendations about what the church should do in response.

The great migration of peasants from the Andean mountains had begun in the 1960s, bringing hundreds of thousands of people into the city. Lima, like many Latin American capital cities, was destined to absorb a large proportion of the country's population as poor rural people "invaded" and organized new urban settlements on the desert sur-

23

rounding the city. Typically, the families started by putting up four *esteras* — reed mats that formed the walls of the dwelling. This was the beginning of a laborious struggle to build a house that often took a decade or longer.

Anyone who has seen the massiveness of poverty in the Lima slums can well understand my sense of bewilderment at the challenge presented to me by the church. However, the vagueness of my job was quite indicative of the level of planning and understanding of the role of the expatriate worker that many missions and volunteer sending organizations had in those days. Unfortunately, there may not have been great improvement in that respect for some of those organizations in the intervening years.

Planning and working out a clear strategy has not been strong in mission organizations. This may be due in part to the individualistic and strong-willed character of many missionaries, though there are, no doubt, many other reasons as well.

FROM DISASTER RELIEF TO RECONSTRUCTION

Incredibly, I was rescued from this vague and overwhelming challenge by one of the most destructive earthquakes to hit Latin America in this century. That calamity struck northern Peru on May 31, 1970, within weeks of our arrival. It resulted in the death of more than sixty thousand people and destroyed tens of thousands of homes, mostly in rural areas in the Andean mountains. Whole towns and villages were destroyed as well as a huge part of the infrastructure, such as irrigation canals, roads, water systems, and communal buildings. One town, Yungay, was literally wiped off the map when a gigantic mud-flow, traveling hundreds of miles an hour from the mountain hovering above, came crashing down upon it. Of a total population of some twenty-two thousand, more than eighteen thousand were buried by the avalanche.

I soon found myself in the midst of a disaster relief program mounted by Church World Service, to which I was loaned from the Lutheran mission with the support of Lutheran World Relief. At that time CWS was "operational" in Peru, set up as a foreign agency to run programs of service, material aid, and development. The term "operational" simply means that CWS did programs themselves as an international agency, rather than working through local organizations. CWS, therefore, was organizationally prepared to mount a large emergency response to the disaster in northern Peru. I was soon to learn also about some of the pitfalls of being operational and carrying out large-scale relief programs.

It should be pointed out that the context of Latin America was different two decades ago in terms of the existence of local nongovernmental organizations capable of doing relief and development work. Today there are dozens of highly qualified Peruvian teams doing work with the poor at the grassroots. In 1970 there were few, if any, that were capable of taking on the scale of relief and reconstruction programs needed in the wake of the 1970 earthquake.

I immediately headed to the earthquake area, where we established a camp on the grounds of the local hospital, the only building that was still standing in the town of Huarmay. One can only imagine what it must have been like to be in an adobe house when the quake hit. The traditional adobe construction is the most common type of building in Andean villages. This type of construction has no reinforcement, and an earthquake easily causes the walls to collapse upon its inhabitants, crushing bones and smothering people as the blocks come crashing down, pulverizing the dry mud.

The first task one encounters immediately after an earthquake is digging people out of the rubble, then binding up wounds and getting the injured to medical help, if possible. Most of the digging out had been done by the time we arrived in the area of quake, but we were able to set up a first aid station and begin to assess damage with the local leaders. Within a short time relief supplies started arriving and we got involved in organizing distribution of food, tools, and tents. Starting the reconstruction work takes planning and, thus, often means delays and frustration for the earthquake victims. There is much scurrying around during this phase, everyone wanting to "do something," but often in an inefficient and uncoordinated way.

FOOD FOR WORK—
DEVELOPMENT OR DEPENDENCY?

In the ensuing months I directed a portion of a disaster response program that channeled hundreds of tons of relief supplies into the earthquake affected area. We began reconstruction projects in dozens of villages in difficult-to-reach and isolated areas of the high Andes. It was here that I had first-hand experience with the famous "food for work" approach to community development. In this case food for work was used for the reconstruction of the physical infrastructure of communities that had been destroyed.

This approach uses food as an incentive for communities to organize and work on self-defined projects, usually building roads, irrigation canals, reservoirs, schools, or community centers. The idea is that the community defines its own needs, contributes some local resources (such as adobe blocks), and organizes teams to work together on the project. The workers are "paid" in food rations depending on the size of their families. This methodology follows the classical community development "felt needs" theory and assumes that this working together will lead to other community betterment projects. However, there are serious problems with food for work.

Food for work projects tend to become rather mechanical and packaged and usually do not include intentional efforts at consciousness raising through an education program. Therefore, what has become known in Latin America as "critical reflection on reality" and grassroots consciousness raising is lacking. The resultant program focuses almost completely on the symptoms rather than causes of communal problems. Of course, this is not all bad in the case of a reconstruction program after an earthquake. The cause of most of the immediate problems of these villages was the earthquake, which had created havoc in their communities.

In principle, these projects stimulate community consciousness and organization, but the great weakness in this approach has been in its dependence on outside resources. As long as the food or other inputs are coming in from the outside, projects get started and carried out. When the aid stops, so do the projects. One thing we started to observe as we visited villages that had been destroyed by the quake, even some weeks or months later, was that the inhabitants often claimed that they had not received any help at all. Even when we knew that material aid had been delivered to people, some inhabitants had learned what to say to outside visitors, especially "gringos" who might be a soft touch and have something to give them. If a sympathetic outsider came to their village, especially someone who was visiting for the first time, he or she would be aghast to hear that these people, who had lost so much, had not received any aid at all! It appears that not only individuals can take on a mendicant attitude, but also whole communities.

DISCONTINUING FOOD PROGRAMS

Often food distribution programs begun in emergency situations are converted to ongoing programs using food for work in community development projects. For years development professionals have debated the effectiveness of this approach. Many have become disenchanted with this method of aid. During the 1980s several of the church-related agencies that formerly had carried out food donation programs in Latin America phased out of them, including Church World Service and Lutheran World Relief. In the late 1980s and early 1990s, even Catholic Relief Services, which was one of the biggest distributors of U.S. government–

donated food, has also been phasing out of this program in Latin America.

The decision to discontinue food distribution programs by these agencies comes about after much internal reflection and debate regarding the benefits and limitations of food distribution. It is also a result of listening to Latin American colleagues in the NGO sector. Many of these partners had became very critical of food programs, even food for work, because of the negative effects it has on popular (people's) organizations. This debate and criticism has been particularly strong in Bolivia, where massive amounts of food are still distributed.

One study criticizes churches and other organizations who run such programs in Bolivia on this point:

> Many of the NGOs and evangelical churches who work in El Alto give food donations without any attempt to build awareness or organization among recipients.... Food-for-work programmes...make no attempt to motivate and engage people concerning the work, so in practice the tasks are not done when the incentives are no longer there.[1]

On the other hand, what should be the proper response of the rich part of the world to such massive disasters as war, earthquakes, or droughts? The natural humanitarian impulse is to send material aid. Nevertheless, those of us who have worked in relief programs have seen real drawbacks in food distribution programs, particularly if too much uncoordinated material aid comes into an area and continues too long. Ongoing food aid is of particular concern, especially because of its tendency to undercut local agricultural production and autonomous community organization. The "D" word, dependency, is certainly one of the biggest quandaries in the aid and development profession and is particularly problematic in food aid programs. Relief and reconstruction programs, while frequently necessary, seldom provide long-term solutions.

During the months I lived in a tent in northern Peru

many community structures and irrigation channels were reconstructed. I never had a chance to revisit those communities in later years, partly because some of that area is now highly "infested" with and controlled by the violent guerilla group called Sendero Luminoso, the Shining Path. It would be interesting to know if that intense period of disaster response and reconstruction had any lasting effect. Nevertheless, as in most cases of disaster programs, after some months we finished our involvement and moved on to other places and challenges. My impression is that we did some good. I hope we did not do any lasting harm to those humble and struggling peasants in the mountains of northern Peru.

IN THE JUNGLE —
WORKING DIRECTLY WITH THE BASE

After about seven months, I returned to the original task of proposing a social development program in which the church could get involved in Peru. Through some contacts and knowledge of what had been going on in the tropical area of Bolivia, I became very interested in the phenomenon of "colonization." This is the term used in the Amazon basin to describe the migration into and settlement on lands in the tropical forests, generally by peasants from the overpopulated highland areas. Sometimes settlers even come from the poverty-ridden populations of the major cities in the region.

In the 1960s and 1970s, the tropics of the Amazon basin countries such as Peru, Bolivia, Brazil, and Ecuador were seen as the great hope for opening up new and productive agricultural lands. Indeed, this migration continues today. Tens of thousands of peasant farmers have left their eroded and worn-out lands in the highlands to settle these areas, using slash-and-burn techniques. They almost never have any prior experience in tropical agriculture, and there is practically no technical assistance available to them. They hear that all they need to do is "put seeds in the ground and anything will grow" in the jungle. Thus, they go about slashing down trees with axes and machetes as if there were no end to the jungle. Trees are seen as the enemy to be eradicated in order to make the jungle produce.

These settlers were often weakened by poor nutrition, malaria, and the steaming heat of the jungle. The obstacles are overwhelming for *colonos*, making the settling of the old West in the U.S. seem like easy ground to hoe.

Colonization of the jungle creates dire ecological consequences. As trees are cut and the soils leached out by heavy rains and the beating sun, these fragile tropical soils become less and less productive with each passing year. As a second growth of brush takes over, the settlers abandon their land and search for another plot of thirty to fifty hectares further into the jungle to start the process all over again.[2]

UN WORLD SUMMIT
ON ENVIRONMENT, 1992

More than twenty years later world consciousness had made a quantum leap from where it was in 1971. The largest United Nations summit ever organized was held in Rio de Janeiro in June 1992 to focus attention on environment and development. One crucial issue discussed there and in many other places today is the matter of sustainable agriculture in the Amazon. One participant in the earth summit who has been working on these issues for many years sees hope for reversing the destruction of the rainforest. He stated, "For one thing government officials in Brazil (and elsewhere) have much more consciousness about the need to support policies and efforts at small-scale sustainable farming. Secondly, it has become very clear from experience that large-scale clearing of the jungle for cattle raising is not economically viable."[3]

COMMUNITY DEVELOPMENT — WHO DOES IT?

In early 1971, the Aaker family moved to live near Pucallpa on the Ucayalli River, one of the uglier towns in the Peruvian jungle. During the next two years I worked at the grass-roots with a group of settlers who had come there to hack a new life out of these tropical forests. These settlers were starting from scratch, had no real pre-existing and viable organization with which to work, and had no experience in the tropics.

We did fish ponds, livestock projects, health teaching, and crops — all along the lines of my best understanding of community development theory and practice. We hired local agronomists to give technical assistance, offered input for concrete projects such as a rustic building for community meetings, and provided materials for a hog house.

We gave special attention to helping the settlers develop leadership for their organization. Church World Service was the funder of this project, and I was thankful to CWS staff for the technical and moral backing they provided me during those months when I often felt quite isolated out there in the jungle.

The approach of this program was along the same lines as countless community development efforts done by Peace Corps Volunteers and other expatriates who try to work directly with grassroots communities. In Latin America this is called working with base communities.

Maybe the times have changed since then, or I have, but looking at that effort in hindsight, I can see the flaws. Today I would seriously question the appropriateness of programs where foreigners try to work directly at the grassroots level. Most programs that place volunteers are relatively short-term, from one to three years. However, it usually takes at least the first year for an outsider to learn the language and understand the culture and even the rudiments of the problems faced by the community. Community development is a long-term process in which the pace of the work should be set by the people themselves. The natural tendency of someone from the outside is to understand progress and problem solving in terms of one's own culture and experience.

There are many "white elephants" strewn across the landscape of low-income countries — often projects initiated by outside resources and persons. There are exceptions where a long-term commitment is made by religious workers, such as priests and nuns, to live with and work by the side of the poor in their own communities.

Nevertheless, one would have to admit that the Peace Corps and other volunteer programs have been a good place to start for those interested in service in the Two-Thirds World. Many of the professionals now working in NGOs and governmental development organizations got their start at the grassroots in some kind of volunteer program. How many times have we heard that those two-year stints were good learning experiences, even though the volunteer did not accomplish much of lasting value?

Certainly, the projects I initiated with that group of settlers had little lasting impact. Within a few years the settlement folded up. The odds were stacked against them. It was just too tough to make it there in the jungle without infrastructural support such as credit and a stronger commitment from government. Most importantly, they did not have the cohesiveness to grow together through the hard times, so they disintegrated as a group and one by one the families deserted the cooperative.

There were some poignant lessons from that experience. First, isolated community development efforts are just that, isolated. They tend not to generate a multiplier effect. Secondly, without a strong commitment on the part of the participants to their own organization, individual projects, even if technically successful, do not necessarily create community or ongoing benefits. Lastly, as mentioned above, this experience brought me to a fundamental re-examination of the role of the development worker and helped me to clarify my assumptions about foreign-supported development programs. It prepared me for the next great challenge that was to present itself very soon, again in the form of an earthquake.

Chapter Three

NICARAGUA
The Right Place at the Right Time

Although we had lived in Latin America for three years, we knew practically nothing about Central America on the eve of its entry into our lives at Christmastime 1972. That was not unusual for most North Americans at that time.[1]

It was only as subversion and revolution spread in that region during the late 1970s that the North American public started to gain some awareness of the people and countries of Central America. And that was due primarily to the fact that U.S. politicians became alarmed about the "communist threat at our own back door."

THE MANAGUA EARTHQUAKE

We had been back in Minnesota from Peru for only a month when we heard the news of the earthquake in Managua. I asked my uncle what he knew about Managua and he sang a little song that had been popular back in the 1940s, "Managua, Nicaragua, Is a Beautiful Town." That was about it, but the difference now was that it was no longer a beautiful town. The earthquake had destroyed most of it.

There was widespread damage, death, and dislocation in the city of Managua. Early estimates of the death toll were in the thousands, and tens of thousands had lost their homes. The final count of the number of deaths from that disaster was never very exact, but estimates went up to sixteen thousand.

The quake that struck Managua on December 23, 1972, did change our lives forever and brought Nicaragua to the attention of the American public for at least a short time. Usually it is the six-o'clock news on television that raises public consciousness in the U.S. about such human tragedy. A destructive earthquake is hot news for a couple of days, maybe with follow-up stories for a couple of weeks. Television is the best fund-raising mechanism that relief agencies have.

Church-related relief and development agencies had not had a significant presence in Central America prior to the Managua earthquake. Agencies like CWS and LWR had supported several programs in South America since the early 1960s, but they had not worked in Central America.

I received a call from Church World Service the day after Christmas, asking me to go to Managua to "mount the CWS response to the earthquake." They anticipated that rather large amounts of funds and material aid would become available very soon.

Five years of prior experience had to be good for something, and I believe it was in this case. My background with emergencies and attempts to organize programs of relief and reconstruction in Vietnam and Peru had been lessons in the school of hard knocks and made me better prepared to respond to this disaster.

In later years I have been asked by young people how one gets into this kind of work and how to make a contribution to the needs of the poor. Part of the answer is that in my case the first five years were for learning. I probably am a slow learner, but I generally advise the young and eager not to expect to make a great contribution or accomplish much their first few years of work in the Two-Thirds World. I believe that in many instances much depends on being the "right person at the right time," which was what happened to me. I just happened to be available. My faith tells me that God had something to do with that, too. Certainly a predisposition to be ready to respond when the need presents itself and as opportunities arise is a requisite for working in this field.

RESPONSE TO A DISASTER

I talked to Church World Service about three conditions for my accepting the challenge of going to Managua. First, I needed as much authority as possible to coordinate the type and pace of the material aid and funds that were to flow in from the churches in the U.S. Second, although there was no existing structure or office in Nicaragua to work through and with, we would not become "operational." We knew very little about what to expect from the churches of Nicaragua, but I wanted to start with them from the beginning and help local churches build something that was theirs. Third, if other expatriates were to become involved, I wanted to have a say in who they were and what their roles would be. Because of some unsavory experiences in Peru, I did not want any unhelpful persons around if I could avoid it.

These conditions were grounded in several principles. One is that the pace, type, and destination of outside resources should be as carefully planned and controlled as possible. Even when the needs and requests are tremendous, it may not be possible to use large amounts of resources in a short period of time. If infrastructure and administrative capacity do not exist, too many resources can ruin a local organization's self-management capacity, especially for an incipient organization. Resources can also lead to corruption and misuse. This is what could be called the saturation principle, and I think it is true for emergency response as well as for development programs.

In the past too many assistance programs in the Two-Thirds World have been "resource driven." They are conceived of and planned on the basis of the availability of funds, materials, and technical assistance from donors. Even though offers of help are motivated by good intentions to help the poor and hungry, this is not the issue. Doing assistance programs with the dignity of the "recipients" in mind is the important point. People who have lost almost everything have the right to participate in deciding what kind of aid is most appropriate and how it should be given.

I witnessed one of the worst examples of this problem in February 1986, when an earthquake devastated countless villages in the highlands in Guatemala. As massive uncoordinated material assistance poured in, attempts to create a local organization of the churches to carry out reconstruction and development programs were totally overwhelmed. Besides encouraging corruption and competition among the leadership with which we were working, much of the material aid that arrived was not in response to a needs assessment done by those in Guatemala. Rather it was based on what people of good will were able to raise as donations in the U.S.

One ideal that has long been held by missionaries and development workers is that of "turning it over to the nationals." History reveals many examples of outside churches and organizations building up institutions, programs, and structures on their own terms and based on their own cultural orientations. When it is time to withdraw and turn it over to a national organization, things start getting complicated. Local leaders may fight over power and resources. Because of inappropriate structures and inadequate local capacity or willingness to assume something that is a foreign imposition, the transfer is fraught with problems. We have seen this happen in numerous places in Latin America. In fact, within a few years we were to run into this very phenomenon in Peru.

I believe the correct principle, when possible, is to start to build something from the beginning that is developed and owned by the people of that country. Especially in this day and age, I do not believe there are many situations in which it is appropriate for a foreign entity to set up its own program, administration, and institution with the intention of "helping the local people." This is especially true for development programs, but the same principle should be followed to the extent possible for emergency relief.

CEPAD: STARTING AN ORGANIZATION

As I headed for Managua the only person whose name I had was Dr. Gustavo Parajón. As it turned out, that was the only one I needed. By the time I got to Managua, Gustavo had already called together some of the pastors of local evangelical (Protestant) churches and met under a tree on the grounds of the mostly destroyed Baptist school. "Evangelical" is the term used in Latin America to describe any kind of church that is not Roman Catholic. In that meeting it was decided to form a committee, which was called CEPAD, the Evangelical Committee for Aid to the Victims. That was the beginning.

Managua was a devastated city, what one imagines the cities of Germany looked like at the close of World War II. This city had the misfortune of being situated directly on top of several geological faults, and the earthquake had gutted its center. In addition to the hundreds of buildings leveled by the quake itself, fires had been ignited by leaking gas mains, causing explosions and more death and destruction. Flights of relief supplies were arriving at Managua's airport by the time I arrived.

When everything has to be done at the same time the problem is where to start. To build a new organization in a rational climate, one has time for planning by objectives, looking at alternative structures, and listening to a variety of opinions. When building an organization and program in the midst of a disaster, with demands coming from dozens of directions every day, one has to rely on other approaches, like crisis management, coordination, and common sense.

The key to the foundation and building of CEPAD was the simple concepts of vision and leadership. Without Gustavo Parajón's leadership ability, sensitivity to the local church environment, and vision, CEPAD would have developed into quite another kind of institution. And it probably would not have lasted.

Twenty years later CEPAD is one of the most dynamic and largest church-related organizations in Latin America.[2] How it got to where it is today is a subject for another book. Nevertheless, I would like to look at several key factors that have led to CEPAD's success and role in the turbulent history of Nicaragua over these last two decades.

GETTING PEOPLE INVOLVED

An earthquake is a terrible human calamity, but it can also be an opportunity for solidarity and compassion. Often it is a mix of human responses, both altruism and greed. On the one hand there are those who take advantage of the misfortune of others by looting, stealing, diverting relief goods, and speculating on land where reconstruction will likely take place. That happened on both a petty and grand scale in the case of Managua. Some of the worst of this corruption was at the hands of the ruling Somoza family and their cronies.

On the other hand, human calamity brings out the best in people and generates empathy and a motivation to help. Though such response can be found in all people irrespective of culture, class, and creed, my observation is that it is a particularly poignant characteristic of poor people and indigenous cultures that have strong community traditions. For example, in Latin American rural communities there is a long tradition of working together in community groups of mutual help. Community work days are a way for people to construct houses, harvest crops, or build roads.

CEPAD was formed by evangelical churches, almost all of them from the "popular" sectors in poor neighborhoods. Within a few days after the formation of CEPAD, we were able to take advantage of this network of congregations to set up children's feeding stations in dozens of poor neighborhoods (*barrios*) around Managua. The principle we followed was to get people involved as soon as possible, not only in helping themselves but also in helping others. We felt we should take advantage of all offers to help. Within a week, this ad hoc coalition of churches was providing daily food to some thirty thousand survivors and pastoral care to many families of the dead.

A corollary principle was not to get stuck in the relief phase. Early on we decided to set a cut-off date for the food distribution effort. Within four months the thirty-two cooperating denominations decided to move from charity for disaster victims to community development with the aim "to help the victims of long-standing poverty and ignorance."[3] To reflect this change in focus, CEPAD changed its name to the Evangelical Committee for Aid to Development, maintaining the same acronym. Direct feeding was discontinued, and CEPAD moved into community-based reconstruction and self-help projects.

We carefully undertook as many reconstruction activities as possible based on the concepts of self-help and community development. The poor were actively involved in the decision making and implementation of projects for their own betterment. CEPAD's 1973 annual report spelled out the role of both urban and rural committees of the poor: defining their own problems, setting goals and planning projects, looking for resources, organizing and working together, and evaluating the results of their efforts. This philosophy, that the best way to help the poor and develop their communities is to mobilize them to help themselves, has remained CEPAD's approach over the intervening years.[4]

INSTITUTION BUILDING

In trying to build an institution such as CEPAD, or any organization dedicated to the work of human development, one of the first challenges is to establish a structure within which programs can be planned and managed. This requires all sorts of management systems, job descriptions, policies on use of resources, and communication channels. At the same time, we worked on a second important task, that of developing competence within the staff, board, and volunteers. Working with poor communities and with people suffering the effects of both natural disasters and human-induced injustice and poverty is one of the most demanding jobs in the world. For all the years I was with CEPAD the work week for employees was typically fifty hours. CEPAD committees and teams spread out into every corner of the country where the needs called them.

People who work in relief and development programs need continuous on-the-job training. In the case of CEPAD, almost none of the staff had any previous experience with this kind of work. Nevertheless, many of them had good innate abilities, positive attitudes, and, perhaps most importantly, high motivation to help people in need.

Though it is not always a guarantee of success to choose people with a "Christian motivation," in the case of CEPAD this was one of the underlying criteria for participation in the program. CEPAD, as a program of the churches of Nicaragua, looked for staff who were motivated by Christian values. This practice seems to have provided a great deal of coherence and an understanding of the broader purpose of the organization. It helped enormously in defining not only what and how the program was to develop, but also why people were involved in it. Leadership training received much attention in the early months and years of CEPAD's life.

THE ROLE OF ADVISOR

These words from an ancient philosopher summarize well the best that an advisor can be:

> Go to the People
> Live with them,
> Learn from them,
> Love them.

> Start with what they know,
> Build with what they have.
>
> But with the best leaders
> When the work is done
>   the task accomplished
> The people will say,
> "We have done this Ourselves."
>
> —Lao Tsu, China, 700 B.C.E.

The role of an advisor can be very broad, or it can be quite specific and technical. However, if the purpose of the advising is organizational development, then one has to be ready for involvement in a myriad of problems and challenges. A paper I wrote in 1976 described the training approach and experiences we had in CEPAD during those years. It delineated some of the main areas in which we undertook the training of leaders and staff. The categories were:

- Planning and organizing

- Human relations and communications

- Management and decision making

- Evaluation

- Skills and knowledge for the job[5]

During my years in Central America, I was involved with CEPAD as an advisor on a full-time basis for several years, and later with other organizations in different countries of the region. The role was always one of working with intermediary organizations, usually church related, to try to help them with planning, program evaluation, staff training, team building, and organizational development. In short, the idea was to help local organizations improve their capacity to run development and outreach programs in service of the poor. My job as an outsider was not directly with the poor at the grassroots.

In order to understand and empathize with the plight of the poor, it was necessary to constantly visit projects and communities, talk with *campesinos* (peasants), community leaders, and urban dwellers, and try to listen to their needs and ideas.

Two principles might be mentioned in relation to the role of advisor. First, one can only be effective in this capacity if one is responding to an invitation and request for help. Part of the job then is to help the organization or team to clearly define its own needs and problems. Next, whenever possible, especially in training situations, a foreigner should work with a local counterpart. A national co-trainer can be much more tuned in to the subtle nuances of language or cultural traits and is usually better able to communicate concepts and tasks in local jargon. Another benefit of working with a counterpart is that of training trainers. Working together we both learn about what works and what does not.

My colleague and friend in LWR/New York, Bob Busche, talked about "low ego needs" as an important attribute for working at the job of advisor (perhaps a better term is "facilitator"). That means being able to get satisfaction out of seeing others do well, without taking credit for accomplishments yourself. The well-worn phrase "working yourself out a job" is an ideal that should be strived for arduously. In the end it may not feel good when you start to realize that you are no longer needed, but you will know you have done your job well.

During more than five years in Central America, I worked with local organizations in Nicaragua, Honduras, Guatemala, and El Salvador as an advisor, trainer, and consultant. For me, one of the keys is to avoid confusing the role of advisor with that of funding agency representative. Those two roles are fundamentally different and conflict if mixed into the same job description. The advisor or facilitator has to work hard at the helping relationship, with objectivity and commitment to the best interests of the people with whom one is working. In the funding agency role, the relationship is influenced by money and all that is implied in donor relations with partner organizations, including feelings associated with power and weakness, trust and mistrust, and asking and giving.

STAYING IN TOUCH WITH THE CHURCHES

One of the criticisms often heard about evangelical churches in Latin America is that they are more interested in gaining members for their flocks than in social service. Evangelicals have gained a reputation of service to their own to the exclusion of others in the community, thereby dividing communities rather than bringing them together. They are also thought of as overly spiritualized, shunning the world and political involvement.

From the first meetings with pastors and leaders of the churches in CEPAD, the importance of being open and nondiscriminatory in service to the whole community was stressed. When a pastor asked in an early meeting if the food being distributed was for the evangelicals, the answer was, "No. The food is for the hungry."

It would have been easier to establish a top-notch technical team for development work, with a rubber-stamp board of directors, than to proceed at the slower pace of the churches. However, in order to be truly an organization of the churches it was important not to move too fast with either program development or pronouncements of what CEPAD stood for. All the issues were present — human rights violations, poverty, injustice, and hunger. They were all dealt with eventually, but not all at once or from the beginning. This may seem contradictory to an outsider with an understanding of the interconnections of all these issues. However, in Latin American churches it is common to shy away from the political implications of justice and human rights. It is easy to identify with the plight of the hungry child or the obvious poverty in urban slums, while ignoring the causes of these situations.

CEPAD's leadership was very conscious of its constituency, aware that the evangelical churches in Nicaragua are conservative and come out of fundamentalist backgrounds. As in all of Latin America, in Nicaragua the growth of the churches has been in the Pentecostal sector, not the mainline historical denominations. It was a great challenge to proceed at the pace of this leadership, many of whom had little formal theological or professional education.

While most organizations set up a board of directors and hold a general assembly once a year, CEPAD held a general assembly of the denominational leaders every month. And what was the agenda? A typical three-hour meeting might dedicate at least half of the time to a Bible study and the rest to discussion of programs and policies. The participation was lively to say the least. CEPAD's leaders were essentially involved in an education and consensus building process that brought the pastors and other leaders to a shared vision of what the organization's mission was and why they were involved in what they were doing.

Seventeen years later CEPAD's assembly decided on another name change, again keeping the same initials for its acronym. CEPAD is now the Council of Evangelical Churches for forty-two denominations. As such CEPAD is an expression of church unity. It continues to respond to emergency needs of floods, war, droughts, and earthquakes. Nicaragua has had more then its share of these over the intervening years. CEPAD also continues as an organization dedicated to development programs through twenty-four local offices in every part of the country. This is how CEPAD defined its purpose at the close of the 1980s:

> We believe that all human beings have been created in God's image, and, therefore, every person is of infinite worth. All persons have the right and, thus, should have the means by which to improve and fulfill themselves....We believe that every person and all groups of people have the right to make economic, religious, political, and other decisions which affect their lives.[6]

Part II

PROMOTING HUMAN DIGNITY

Present global economic, political, and environmental trends present formidable challenges. Time is running out for a world overburdened by population growth, environmental deterioration, and violent struggle for survival. The de-humanizing poverty that affects so many millions in the world today needs to be urgently addressed on both macro and micro levels. We need to look at our priorities for the use of limited resources of this world.

SYMPTOMS OR CAUSES

Analyzing the causes of poverty, hunger, and violence and forging strategies to confront them locally and globally must be a major part of the agenda of concerned citizens of both the North and the South in these last years of the twentieth century and on into the twenty-first. It is no longer a viable option to put most of our efforts into treating the symptoms of poverty and hunger, while the causes go unaddressed.

Among these causes are external debt and unfavorable terms of trade, militarization, exploitation by the powerful, environmental degradation, and overpopulation. Probably it is of equal importance to mention good, old-fashioned greed, selfishness, and lack of vision. Just note a few relevant statistics that reflect on priorities:

- In 1988, UNICEF estimated that 500,000 children had died in the previous year as a direct result of poor countries' debt service payments to richer nations.

- One-third of the world's land surface, on which almost one-fifth of humanity lives, is threatened with desertification.

- In tropical areas, developers and low-income settlers are cutting down the forests at the rate of 40 to 50 million acres every year, an area the size of Washington State.

- In the United States we spend over $100,000 a year for each soldier, while less than $1,000 in Federal aid is spent on each student.

A Church World Service study describes some of the dire statistics of children in low-income countries:

There are now 100 million street children worldwide, and of these, 50 percent are located in Latin America and the Caribbean. In Bolivia, 1,037,500 children are marginalized from school and therefore will be illiterate. Ninety percent of these are girls. In Port-au-Prince, Haiti, 5,000 children live in the streets; 85 percent are ignorant as to who their fathers are.[1]

ALLEVIATING POVERTY: SOME MODELS

Since World War II there have been several schools of thought regarding the best way to help the poor through development assistance programs. The 1950s and 1960s were greatly influenced by the heady experience of having reconstructed Europe through the Marshall Plan. The same strategy of input to get industry and agriculture going in low-income countries did not, however, follow that pattern.

Infusions of modern technology, infrastructure, and industry, while stimulating a certain degree of economic growth on a macro level, did not trickle down to benefit the poor and improve their living conditions.

In a survey of the predominant theories of development that have influenced academics and development professionals over the last several decades, Wayne Bragg lists several.[2] He maintains that the dominant approach to raising the standard of living and providing the most good to the maximum number of people has been modernization. Its ultimate goal is to increase production and economic growth through the transfer of knowledge, technology, and capital from the "advanced" nations.

The 1970s saw a reaction to this theory, perhaps in some degree in response to the increasing clamor from the masses of poor that were growing in numbers and making demands for a more just share of the world's economic pie. The prevalent strategy for poverty alleviation in the 1970s has been called the "reformist doctrine" by John Lewis. He says that donors "sought to mount direct attacks on poverty that would not necessarily displace but augment macro development efforts."[3] Some of the catchwords of the decade were "redistribution with growth," "basic needs," and the "poorest of the poor." Stress was placed on development projects that were specifically aimed at a particular locality and population.

FOUR OPTIONS FOR HELPING THE POOR

The Spanish term *promoción humana* is widely used in Latin America when talking about helping people who live in conditions of great human need. Though it is difficult to come up with an exact translation, the concept is similar to the North American idea of social service and outreach to people in poverty. *Promoción humana* is applied to a wide variety of approaches to helping. While it can include direct services and welfare, it usually refers to the idea of people taking responsibility to work toward their own social and economic development.

Those of us in the "developed world" often think in fairly concrete and material terms when we define our understanding of helping people living in poverty. However, experience in Latin America has taught us that it is of equal or more importance to consider intrinsic values such as dignity, solidarity, and community when setting a course of accompanying the poor.

Frances O'Gorman, a Brazilian who has worked for many years with marginalized people in areas of extreme poverty in her country, has developed a very helpful scheme for conceptualizing various approaches of *promoción humana*. O'Gorman talks about (1) direct assistance, (2) the teaching approach, (3) development projects, and (4) transformation. Each of the four models she describes is valid and appropriate in specific settings, but there are certain limitations inherent in each approach as well.

On the one hand, there are the risks of paternalism and dehumanization in helping relationships. On the positive side there is also the potential in each approach for a relationship based upon dignity.

Attempts to help the poor are influenced by many factors, most of them having to do with our perception of the world and our motivation for helping.[4] First we need to examine our assumptions about why people are poor and who they are. The reality in which poor people live can be explained in various ways, including social, political, spiritual, or economic. Our reactions to conditions of injustice and poverty are, in turn, influenced by our values as well as our skills and sensitivities in dealing with injustice and poverty.

In the following chapters we will take a look at the four above-mentioned approaches to helping the poor.

Chapter Four

HOW DO WE SPELL RELIEF?

Helping the Poor through "Assistance"

On a global scale at the beginning of the 1990s around 100 million people are completely homeless, some 800 million go hungry every day, and more than a billion survive in absolute poverty. Children and women suffer the most. Some 40 million newborns are not properly immunized. Fourteen million children under the age of five die each year and 150 million are malnourished.[1]

As I write these words the American public is being bombarded by images of disasters and human suffering in many parts of the world. There were 2 million Kurdish refugees from Iraq in the aftermath of the Gulf war; cyclones and tidal waves once again battered Bangladesh and killed 150,000 people; war and famine have put some 27 million people at risk of starvation in Ethiopia, Sudan, Somalia, Liberia, Mozambique, Angola, and elsewhere in Africa; a cholera epidemic swept through Peru; a volcano erupted in the Philippines and simultaneous earthquakes and storms affected tens of thousands of people. Many persons have even experienced a kind of "disaster fatigue" in the face of this seemingly endless barrage of international calamities.

MERCY AND CHARITY

Being merciful and expressing charity as concretely as possible is the most common type of help extended to the poor and downtrodden. There is a long tradition of responding to human need by direct assistance or humanitarian aid, especially within Christian churches. We find many calls in Scripture to respond to God's desire for us to meet basic needs. The prophet Isaiah asks, "Is not this what I require of you as a fast... to set free those who have been crushed? Is it not sharing your food with the hungry, taking the homeless poor into your house, clothing the naked?"

For the compassionate, those who are poor and in need of help include beggars, the sick, the hungry, the abandoned, and the homeless. They are the castaways of society, forgotten and living in precarious circumstances, virtually unable to survive without outside help. They are seen as unable to feed themselves because of natural or human caused disasters or unable to fend for themselves because they are refugees from political and military turmoil. In today's world large numbers of the human family fall into this category of human need.

Anyone who has walked the streets of a major city in a low-income country and has encountered the outstretched hands of beggars or seen lame and blind people on the roadside has had to deal personally with the question of whether or not to give help. In recent years this face-to-face encounter with the poor has become ever more common on the streets of our major cities in the North as well.

On a larger scale, institutions set up to do relief work have to make decisions about where, how much, and to which human tragedy among many they should respond.

In industrialized societies such as the United States, the average citizen does not often encounter face to face such extreme degrees of human need. We are more likely to be confronted by human suffering through the written word, television, and fund appeals asking us for donations for relief to the hungry and poor. Nor do average North Americans go directly to the aid of the poor and hungry. Rather they support a "charity" of choice, sending checks to organizations that they feel are able to deliver the most direct assistance to the needy with the least amount of overhead. In fact, many times the hard questions dealing with why there is so much poverty and hunger are not asked. Likewise, the more obvious question of how much of the aid actually gets to the hungry can just as easily be overlooked by those responding to advertisements that pull at the heart strings.

HUNGER RELIEF

The special "hunger appeals" that many church denominations have set up often appeal to this level of compassion. It is a very human response to want to help the "least of these," and relief is the most easily understood type of help. Most church members and citizens want our institutions and governments to be responsive to the needs of the destitute. Indeed, Christians find in the Bible a logical relationship between faith and action. The apostle James makes one of the strongest linkages between faith and the supplying of basic physical needs to others in a direct way. This, he says, is an expression of true faith:

> Suppose a brother or sister is in rags with not enough to eat for the day, and one of you says, "Good luck to you, keep yourselves warm, and have plenty to eat," but does nothing to supply their bodily needs, what is the good of that? So with faith, if it does not lead to action, it is in itself a lifeless thing. (James 2:15–16)

It is probably the image of relief that comes to the minds of most people when they think of the work of their favorite charity. Members of churches get involved in a physical way in this kind of aid, making and donating quilts or health kits and donating used clothes, soap, or money.

Into the decade of the 1990s LWR, for example, continued to be heavily involved in relief programs in sub-Sahara Africa.[2] Toward that end LWR and other church-related agencies received large amounts of resources from the United States government for channeling to relief programs. Most of the money received from private contributions goes to development programs. In spite of the large proportion of resources that these agencies report as expended in relief programs, professional staff of these agencies would probably unanimously say that they spend most of their time and creative energies thinking about and working on long-term development alternatives.

ARE HUNGER AND POVERTY GETTING WORSE?

There are more hungry people in the world today then ever before, and there appear to be more disasters with each succeeding decade, resulting in increasing numbers of victims in need of humanitarian aid.[3] Statistics show that during the 1970s, six times as many people died from "natural disaster" each year as in the 1960s. Droughts and floods, disasters caused by widespread deforestation and overcultivation, increased most in terms of numbers affected. The trends have continued to accelerate during the 1980s, with droughts in Africa, India, and Latin America and floods throughout Asia. The 1990s has ushered in a decade of possibly even greater catastrophes. One human tragedy after another overwhelms our senses on television. We can hardly take in the meaning and scope of the Kurdish refugee problem before the next news items shows scenes from one of the most devastating cyclones in the history of Bangladesh.

Some of the most dramatic examples of this level of human need are seen in the least developed countries of Africa south of the Sahara, where massive humanitarian assistance from the international community has been required during the 1980s and into the 1990s. Particularly staggering have been the situations in Ethiopia, the Sudan, and

Somalia. The growing numbers of refugees and hungry people in the world, created by war and conflict, are alarming and show little indication of subsiding. Larry Minear wrote in reference to the Sudan tragedy, "The scale of suffering during the mid-eighties was staggering. UN figures put the number of southerners (in Sudan) displaced during 1986–88 at some three million.... Deaths during the years 1986–88 are placed between 400,000 and 500,000 persons. The UN estimates deaths related to war and famine in 1988 alone at 250,000. Half of these were children."[4]

IS HUMANITARIAN ASSISTANCE NONPOLITICAL?

There are very few actions in this world of inequitable relations that are neutral. Any kind of aid intervention has political overtones, even when the helping agent wants to stay clear of politics. The wisest course is to steer away from partisan politics while recognizing the very political nature of all we do in the name of relief and development.

The Ethiopian situation is a good case in point. As one observer commented,

Good intentions are not an appropriate foundation for good programs. Agencies' attempts to ignore the context of the Ethiopian famine by burying their heads in the sand and claiming political neutrality cannot be accepted. Finding out as much information as possible about the situation in which it is directly involved is an agency's only hope for remaining neutral. Each relief and development agency operating in Ethiopia is political, each has its own agenda, albeit hidden, its own ideological leanings and its own assumptions about what constitutes appropriate relief and development activities. Is it possible to give nonpolitical, humanitarian assistance? In an absolute sense, probably not. However, the best way to remain neutral in such situations is to keep informed.[5]

Central America during the 1980s demonstrated how assistance can exacerbate social conflicts between the poor and the rich. Assistance provided in inappropriate ways can actually have the negative effect of strengthening the rich. Government-to-government aid is frequently criticized for reinforcing or even worsening the status of the poor vis-à-vis more privileged sectors of society through which such aid flows.[6]

CAN ONE PERSON MAKE A DIFFERENCE?

Mother Teresa of Calcutta is a world-recognized symbol of compassion and of the direct-assistance approach to human promotion. Her mission to the poorest of the poor has been universally admired, winning her a Nobel peace prize in 1979. Mother Teresa's Christian faith and her love for the poor is the motivation for her practice of direct assistance. She says,

> Everything is done on the basis of the needs of the poor....If they ask for bread, we give it to them. If there is no one to wash their clothes, we wash them. ...If there are orphans, we build an orphanage. If we find abandoned people in the streets, we rescue them. ...Our mission understands the problem in more individual terms then collectively. We take care of each person, not the multitudes.[7]

Regarding her philosophy of help, Mother Teresa said, "I have been asked many times if, rather than giving a fish to the hungry, we should not give them a fishing pole so that they can catch the fish themselves. My God! Many times they do not even have the strength to hold the fishing pole, so we have to give them fish today to help them recuperate enough strength to be able to catch fish tomorrow."[8]

For the compassionate ones, the "assistance" approach to human need, which is also called welfare, relief, or humanitarian aid, means providing financial and material resources

or human attention to directly meet the needs of the poor.
Help is motivated from feelings of charity, humanitarianism,
and religious obligation to do something to mitigate the effects of human suffering. This is a testimony of love toward
one's neighbor, acted out in giving the cup of cold water to
the thirsty and bread to the hungry.

Usually the relationship in the assistance model is in one
direction, from the giver to the receiver, whether the help is
in the form of aspirins, milk, clothes, or personal caring for
the needs of the body.

ONE CHURCH'S RESPONSE

For some years the Lutheran Church in El Salvador, with
support from Lutheran World Relief and various other agencies, has worked in programs of assistance to displaced
people. Bishop Medardo Gómez has demonstrated great
courage and prophetic vision in his leadership of the Lutheran Church as he has tried to live in faithfulness to the
Gospel. The following is an account I wrote of that program
in 1983:

> The displaced people of El Salvador are living the most
> perilous life imaginable. Caught in the cross fire of war,
> many have had to flee for their lives, often hiding for
> a time in the hills and eventually reaching an urban
> area where there may be some hope for survival. In
> the urban areas they find little reason for hope — no
> jobs, no housing, and often not enough food or basic
> necessities to keep them alive.
>
> On one visit to a refugee barrio we visited a shack
> where we found four children. The oldest, about six
> or seven years old, was caring for his younger siblings.
> The youngest was a baby lying in a pile of rags on
> the only piece of furniture in the shack, a makeshift
> bed. The parents were out looking for work, food, fire-
> wood, or whatever they would need to survive until

tomorrow. The condition of the baby made me doubt that the parents would have many more days to worry about providing for him.

Five months later I visited El Salvador again and went with the Lutheran team to the refugee camp, now known as "Faith and Hope." The children were gathered together and as they sang for us with loud and exuberant voices, and as the women expressed their gratitude for what "we had done for them," I was moved to tears. In fact, these refugees, with the help of the Lutherans of El Salvador, had done much to help themselves. Now they ran their own camp, one group doing food preparation, another producing food on the plot of land around the buildings by planting vegetables and corn, another in charge of cleanliness and health.

Besides doing relief it is important, too, to raise a prophetic voice in our own country where political decisions affecting the lives of Central Americans are made. As we come to understand more fully the suffering of our Central American brothers and sisters, we, as North Americans, will see our connection with the Central American tragedy.

The Lutherans of San Salvador are only one example of the Church in Central America as it works to do justice and show compassion and mercy to the downtrodden. That Church is humbly living its commitment to the poor through the unity of the body of Christ.[9]

HUMANITARIAN ASSISTANCE AND JUSTICE

Mother Teresa and her co-workers and the Lutheran Church in El Salvador are examples of humanitarian assistance. They seem to be engaged in the same kinds of activities in response to human need — feeding the hungry and binding up broken bodies — and both, in my opinion, are meritorious examples of Christian compassion. However, by their pronouncements, Bishop Medardo Gómez and Mother Teresa reveal differing understandings of the role of a Christian in response to human suffering.

Bishop Gómez has clearly placed himself and the church in El Salvador on the side of the poor in the face of the structural violence and injustice perpetrated by the powerful. This is a risky position to take and one that has led to threats, arrests, torture, and the death of some of those who have followed that path.

These two exemplary figures have made a difference as individuals in their sojourn of service to the poor. Bishop Gómez has chosen to be both a prophetic voice for justice and a compassionate giver of assistance. Both have chosen to uplift the dignity and sacredness of each human being, giving totally of themselves in their service.

LIMITATIONS OF THE ASSISTANCE APPROACH

Often those who practice the assistance approach do not question the causes of the human need and suffering. There are fewer risks of doing something controversial in this approach, but the action often leaves one wondering if or how the real problem can or should be addressed.

The assistance relationship is one to one or one to an anonymous population, and the aid is given on the criterion of need. Often the aid giver does not even know the language or historical context of the ones to whom help is being given.

No matter how much the helper loves the poor and identifies with them, he or she cannot "be one of them," except in the rare case of a Mother Teresa who takes the mandate of spiritual poverty literally. We cannot know, in the deepest sense, what it means to live the life of poverty. Most people who are motivated to help the poorest and most destitute have to admit that they would be unable to survive on the edges of society as the poor do. Normally help is given from a distance.

The assistance approach to human promotion is concerned with remedial action, without the need to interfere with the way society is organized. In fact, the person who wants to help can be part of the problem as well as the solution. The compassionate one does not necessarily question the way society is structured, but does feel that it is necessary to give generously to those who are injured and made destitute by that society or by other forces beyond the control of the poor.

Though not depreciating the need for and possibilities of providing direct humanitarian assistance, we should raise questions about the sufficiency of this approach. How to express love very concretely in an indifferent and unjust world is a question worthy of much reflection by caring people. Giving aid to those in desperate situations is a necessary human and Christian act.

We are left with many unanswered questions. From years of involvement in and observation of direct assistance programs, I have come to the conclusion that although relief is not enough, it is often a necessary response. It is an obligation, really, of people of conscience.

Chapter Five

IS KNOWLEDGE ENOUGH?

The Education Approach to Helping the Poor

Education: From the Latin *educere,* to lead out

A second approach to helping the poor is through teaching. The underlying assumption here is that by learning skills and gaining knowledge the poor will be able to take advantage of the means available to them in society to better their condition. This is the "pull yourself up by your own bootstraps" theory of human promotion.

Those who would help the poor through teaching assume that people who lack education (i.e., knowledge or skills) do not know how to help themselves. They are, therefore, left behind or out of the mainstream. They are the stragglers of society. It is, however, possible for stragglers to learn to become useful citizens, according to the teachers.

The teachers recognize that to give a person a fish satisfies her or his hunger for a day, but the solution to satisfying the hunger of a lifetime comes through teaching the poor to catch fish for themselves. The assumption upon which this approach is based, namely, that learning to catch fish will provide food or income, does not necessarily address more complex questions of justice. For example, what if a factory up the river has contaminated the water so badly that the

59

fish are dying? Or what if people living near the river do not have fishing rights?

WHO ARE THE POOR?

How do those who choose the teaching approach understand poverty? The poor are poor because of ignorance, apathy, or lack of opportunity. The poor are those who do not complete school; they are exploited child laborers, the unskilled and underemployed who sell pencils on the street corner, begging street children and young women who sell their bodies to survive. They are women who are discriminated against because of their sex. They are indigenous people (Indians or other minorities) who have been left behind by the dominant society and have not been completely incorporated into society by an education system that is designed for and by the majority.

Take note of some statistics about the conditions of millions of poor people in the Two-Thirds World. (The term "South" here refers to low-income countries.)

- There still are about 100 million children of primary school age in the South not attending school.

- Nearly 900 million adults in the South are illiterate.

- The female literacy rate in the developing countries is only two-thirds that of males.

- 150 million children under five (one in every three) suffer from serious malnutrition.[1]

In the past some organizations, such as CARE and Operation Bootstrap, have given much support to programs that build school classrooms. Nevertheless, these organizations have seen that the classroom is only one of the elements lacking in poor communities. On countless visits to rural communities in Latin America, I have seen that the schoolteacher is much more crucial. Urban teachers are very often assigned by the government to rural schools even though they may not really want to live in the countryside. They commute back and forth from city to country, often arriving in the community on Monday afternoon and leaving for home in the city around Friday noon. The students are shortchanged, and the parents often have no control or way to hold the teacher accountable. In addition, the lack of even rudimentary materials and books is endemic in poor communities, reinforcing a system of education that relies on rote memory, repetition, and copying notes from the blackboard.

Opportunities for education in rural areas of the Two-Thirds World are almost always less than in urban centers. Traditionally, children begin to help with agriculture and livestock care at a very young age. By the time they have gone through three years of primary school, which is usually all that is available in their community, they become full-time contributors to the family labor force. Their formal education is over at an early age. From then on books and reading materials are almost never available to them for continuing to explore the world of ideas. In one case in Mexico,

> Only about 60 per cent of children finish primary school here and only 25 per cent join secondary schools. Teachers are badly paid and so badly motivated and there is an 80 per cent shortage of basic textbooks. (Father Antonio, headmaster, San Miguel Teotongo)[2]

APPROPRIATE EDUCATION

The question remains: "What is gained if people are taught to catch fish if there are no jobs in the fishing industry?" Teaching skills and knowledge is one side of the equation. Another important goal of teaching should be to build dignity and enhance self-determination.

Almost all development projects in Latin America supported by church development agencies contain a strong component of training, with the emphasis on "appropriate" content and methods. The training usually reinforces two important areas of the project, organization and production. Thus, the education effort is aimed at consciousness raising and empowerment as well as increasing technical capacities to improve living conditions. Perhaps the most effective approach to training that has been developed in the last several decades is that of training community-level promoters. This has been a particularly strong feature of primary healthcare programs in communities that lack medical facilities and attention.

Communities select one or two leaders to receive training in some of the basics of health, and they return to work under a local committee on preventive and curative health care in their own community. As leaders pass on new knowledge and concepts to their neighbors the multiplier effect is quite astounding; moreover, the program has a low cost. One very effective example of this approach is that of PROVADENIC, a primary health program headed by Dr. Gustavo Parajón in Nicaragua. This project has consistently helped to keep infant mortality and malnutrition down in several dozen rural communities in that country for many years.

One of the biggest problems we have had with training programs is in evaluation of effectiveness. Even though almost everyone feels that training is important, it is very difficult to know with some degree of certainty what the results and effects of that training are.

Some international agencies have brought trainees to the U.S. for advanced professional or technical training in settings completely different from those of their home countries. In the end we have to ask ourselves if the large effort we make in training has really helped the poor. Is it appropriate training? A difficult question to answer.

Vocational education, technical assistance, and extension services are expressions of the teaching approach to human promotion. Under this approach it is thought that those who have access to information and skills can instruct those who lack access to the knowledge necessary to earn a living in society. Thus, through teaching, these "nonmembers" are motivated and equipped to become members of society, to fit into and take advantage of the benefits of society.[3] Yet, with massive unemployment and crippled economies in many low-income countries, training has not always been enough.

POPULAR EDUCATION

In the 1960s churches and nongovernmental organizations in the Two-Thirds World, particularly in Latin America, started to use the term "popular education" to designate a method to achieve social and political change. The popular education approach adapts itself to the community and not the community to a method developed elsewhere. Adult literacy was an intricate part of this movement.

The Spanish word *popular* is not equivalent to the same English word. The sense in which it is used in the grassroots movements in Latin America is "of the people" rather than "liked by many people." Popular education means an education that is of the people and appropriate to their needs, culture, and historical context.[4]

For education to be effective the teacher must relate to people's potential and to their capacities to develop themselves. The teacher should avoid reinforcing feelings of inferiority or low self-esteem. Rather, people need to know their value as human beings, where they stand in relation to others, their culture, and their community.

David Thorp, who spent many years living with his family in a shantytown outside of Lima, Peru, used the popular education model in his work with base Christian communities. He describes popular education this way:

> Education is either designed to maintain the existing situation, imposing on the people the values and

culture of the dominant society, or education is designed to liberate people, helping them to become
critical, creative, free, active and responsive members
of society.

In Latin America the 1970s saw the growth of the
consciousness-raising school of thought as a key, though controversial, method for working with grassroots movements.
Concientización, as advocated by Paulo Freire, implies an educational process whereby people discover their own reality
and act upon newfound awareness of their situation, i.e.,
liberating education.

Early in his career, Freire became involved in church programs as a way of addressing social problems and poverty in
northeast Brazil. Before long he became aware of the contra-
dictions involved in charity work, in which the benevolent
middle class would do things for the poor but not with
them. He turned to adult literacy, a critical issue at the time
because illiterate people were not allowed to vote. Freire
became famous for his efforts to incorporate critical thinking into literacy teaching as a way to raise consciousness in
people about their own reality.[5]

One notable practitioner of liberating education was
Bishop Leónidas Proaño, who did pastoral work in Rio-
bamba, Ecuador, for thirty-one years. He dedicated his life
to the marginal people in his diocese and became known
as the "bishop of the Indians." Proaño said that "when we
speak of a liberating education, we cannot speak of educators and pupils, but have to place ourselves at the same
level. The *campesinos* [peasants] are educators as much as
we are, and we are also as much pupils as the *campesinos* are. I would even dare emphasize that we are the
ones who most need to raise our consciousness; that is
to say, to reach the point of being able to feel, to experience the pain, the suffering, the uncertainty that the
campesino experiences in his daily life."[6] In the best sense
of the word, teaching and learning are two-directional and
reciprocal.

RAISING CONSCIOUSNESS IN THE NORTH

During the 1980s and into the 1990s a large number of people from northern countries have participated in study tours to southern countries. These experiences give people the opportunity to encounter poverty conditions and poor people on a personal level. Among the most common reactions of participants on these tours are comments like these: "I learned a lot — they have much to teach us," or "For the first time I see the connection between the way we live in the North and conditions of injustice and poverty in the South." I quote an excerpt from a report I wrote after such a tour to Central America, which reflects this reaction:

> On this sojourn we met a few representatives of the millions of poor in Latin America. They were our teachers.... They were a refugee, a campesino leader, a village midwife, the head of a group of the families of the "disappeared," a rural pastor, a delegate of the word. They are the people who Gustavo Gutiérrez tells us are moving from becoming "non-persons" to becoming persons. They are giving rise to a new way of being a person and a believer, a new way of living and thinking the faith, a new way of being summoned, and summoning the Church — *La Iglesia* — the assembly of those called together for mission. They invited us to join them in that mission. They taught us about mission.

The study tour can be an intense educational experience, though limited to relatively few participants. Finding ways to multiply these experiences is crucial. One of the keys to bringing about a more equitable and just world lies in educating people in the North about the causes of poverty and injustice in the South. In the long run changes in the North may be of more importance than development programs aimed at teaching technical or administrative skills to the poor. Methods of popular education being worked out in the

South can be used in the North to build the consciousness needed to bring about these changes.

LIMITATIONS OF THE TEACHING APPROACH TO HELPING THE POOR

Many education systems and schools in the Two-Thirds World utilize a rote memory and "banking" approach to teaching. Through written notebooks and tests, the student is expected to regurgitate the information "deposited" by the teachers. In addition, most classrooms are overcrowded and underequipped in poor countries, making for a low-quality education.

One positive feature of the teaching approach is that it can be an effective instrument to help the underprivileged to defend themselves so as to raise themselves out of the condition of poverty. Nevertheless, one of the limitations is that those who are in charge of teaching control information and exercise an influence on how reality is interpreted. If done in a paternalistic way, the teacher can promote conformism and submission. The teaching approach itself does not change the social and economic context in which the "trained" person lives.

In the decades of the 1950s and 1960s there was great enthusiasm for change through technical and professional training, to bring the "backward," preindustrial countries into the modern age. However, many people were educated for jobs that did not exist and for social and economic expectations that were unrealistic.

The teaching approach to human promotion has been heavily used by church missions, with the view to help the poor by setting up schools to produce leaders for society. Both Catholic and Protestant missions invested significant resources into building institutions in their "mission fields." Some have later evaluated these programs in the light of their effect on society, particularly their helpfulness to the less fortunate. An example from Brazil:

Photo: John Workman

El Salvador: Author Jerry Aaker, Bishop Medardo Gomez, and Dr. Angel Ibarra meet in a temporary shanty town. In the early 1980's tens of thousands of rural families fled their homes because of war and oppression. The Salvadoran Lutheran Church and relief organizations banded together to help in relief and rehabilitation.

Vietnam: Earl Martin, Mennonite Central Committee volunteer, and Tharon McConnel of Church World Service in a refugee camp near Quan Ngai giving aid to Vietnamese citizens made homeless by the war. Relief organizations worked through the Vietnam Christian Service coalition to meet the people's needs.

Children in the rain forest area of the Amazon basin have learned to plant trees to help save their environment and the world's. Here they demonstrate their skill to author Jerry Aaker.

Bolivia: In community development, people are encouraged to define their own priorities. In the arid highlands and the tropics, water is often a major need. Canadian Lutheran World Relief helps communities in this area put in wells like the one pictured above.

Bolivia: Learning how to read and write is a high priority among women in the rural Andean region. Becoming minimally literate is a concrete step giving women a greater sense of dignity.

Honduras: Children are often fed in emergency programs set up after hurricanes or other disasters. Organizations like Heifer Project International help people produce their own food so that long term feeding programs become unneces

Peru: A community meeting outside a rural church in the southern highlands. Many Latin American churches, both Protestant and Catholic, are important centers where activities promoting justice for the poor and oppressed take place.

Peru: Demonstrators in Ayaviri, Peru protest the high cost of living resulting from government policy.

Honduras: This family is one of a group of landless people who have begun to produce their own food in an unused area that they have occupied.

Photo: Rosa Villa Fuerte

Peru: A small child is sheltered by
her mother during a march in Lima
protesting the halt to a feeding
program that had provided a glass
of milk per day for each child.

Photo: Tafos Workshop

Peru: Violence by the "Shining Path" rebels and counter attacks by the military have escalated the tragedy in Peru. Scenes like the funeral of a community leader shown above are quite common.

Cover photo:
A Salvadoran family, part of the La Florida Co-operative project supported by the Episcopal Church of El Salvador. Many of the participants were later killed in a night of terror.
Photo: John Workman

Since the beginning of evangelization work in Brazil, the evangelical churches founded schools, orphanages, hospitals, and other institutions of a social, economic and religious character in this country. However, many of these institutions have stopped reflecting the Gospel. Instead, primary and secondary schools as well as universities have been used by the upper classes to prepare the elites for positions of power in our society.... In what way do these institutions open their doors to the least favored of our society?... How can our institutions give service and attention to the Brazilian people without turning our back on the mission of the church?[7]

Teaching is certainly a valid method for human promotion, especially when teachers and facilitators of this approach take seriously the felt and real needs of the people they are teaching. Both learner and teacher need to be in a mutual search for alternatives and answers, open to discovery and with a healthy respect for native wisdom and values. If this is the attitude of the helper and if the goal is not only to help one person among thousands to fish, but to work for better conditions for the whole fishing community, then teaching is at least part of the solution for the poor.

Chapter Six

THE PARTICIPATION PRINCIPLE

Promoting Participatory Development

Giving direct assistance and teaching are two forms of helping the poor. Nevertheless, many who work in human promotion believe that these methods do not address the complexities of the underlying causes of poverty. Thus, there has been a strong emphasis by many development agencies to work with the poor and oppressed by helping them discover their own path of participation and to reclaim their rights within society.

Those who take the option of promoting participation see the poor as those who have been forced to live at the margins of society. Marginalized people have little access to the goods and services provided by society and have fewer opportunities to be productive and self-reliant. If they have work, they receive miserly pay; if their children go to school, the education is not suited to their needs and many drop out because of economic pressures; they are forced off fertile lands and have to subsist on small plots (*minifundios*) of often degraded soils; when they organize to demand their rights they are seen as subversives; they have little voice in the dominant political system in their country.

In the 1970s I often visited rural communities in Nicaragua where CEPAD was working with development projects. Typically we needed to drive for miles through fertile bottom land planted in sugar cane before we reached the stark, eroded hillsides where the *campesinos* scratched out a meager living. The thousands of acres of sugar cane were connected to the main highway by paved roads, while the marginal land in the hills was accessible only during the dry season over dirt roads. The term "marginal" was never more clearly demonstrated to me.

The *campesinos* were literally pushed to the margins of the good land by the powerful Somoza family, who owned the sugar cane fields. Everything about the lives of those *campesinos* was marginal. They had the worst land, no credit, poor transportation, no salable skills, and no political power (until they organized in support of the Sandinista revolution).

Who are marginalized people? Lutheran World Relief defines them this way:

> The term "marginal communities" aptly describes the groups or communities LWR shall assist. This term refers to communities of people in localities or countries who are unable, de facto, to participate beneficially in the dominant economic, social and political systems. Living at the margin of human existence, they are unable to influence or change the systems which effectively thwart their efforts to meet their basic human needs. Such communities are marked by widespread poverty, hunger, malnutrition, illness, unemployment, low life expectancy, high infant mortality, lack of educational opportunity or other means of improving their condition.[1]

In Matthew 25, Jesus sets forth a great ethical challenge to his followers to take seriously the fundamental needs of the poor — food, water, shelter, clothing, health care, and spiritual nurture. Very serious words, indeed, for they are used in Jesus' message about salvation on the final judgment day. The mandate from Scripture is clear.

WHAT IS DEVELOPMENT?

Development: from the Latin *de (dis-, apart)* and the French *voloper* (to wrap), i.e., to unwrap or uncover.[2]

The focus on marginal communities arises from a motivation to help the poor in meeting their most basic life-sustaining needs, and this leads agencies like LWR to provide for these basic needs directly through assistance (relief). It also leads to an emphasis on work through development projects. LWR's definition of development, no doubt heavily influenced by the above Scripture reference and others, is the following:

> Development is a process by which people collectively address and seek to mitigate the causes and consequences of poverty, hunger, sickness, ignorance and injustice. Its aim is to achieve more fully the God-given human potential of all community members, creating more caring and just communities in which all members have access to means for meeting their basic human needs for food, shelter, clothing, employment, health care and human development.[3]

PROMOTING PARTICIPATION THROUGH ACCOMPANIMENT

Participation has become the fundamental principle followed by development practitioners. Those who believe in this philosophy make a commitment to *accompany* marginated people as they work out their own solutions to their most basic problems. *Accompaniment* means a commitment to walking with rather than doing for.

In North America the term "development" is often used in reference to building houses or shopping malls. It is also commonly used in relation to fund raising and the putting together of a new product line, as in "research and development." However, when we use the term in reference to programs of human promotion through participation, we are talking about processes in which the people themselves organize and define their own needs, work to overcome obstacles they face as a community, and take responsibility for their own social and economic future. The concept goes beyond strictly technical and economic definitions. It is the "uncovering" of their own potential as communities and as people.

In the participatory approach it is not the individual that is the focus of attention, as is usually the case in the assistance and teaching approaches. Rather, the people's organization is promoted, whether that be at the community level, an association, a cooperative, or a base Christian community. The needs of each individual and family are important, and what each brings to the community is valuable. But the commitment here is to work for the good of self *and* others — through the community and for the community's well-being.

Those who are committed to participation promote consciousness raising and try to help the marginated to claim their rights and regain self-esteem. Staff and volunteers of development agencies have literally thousands of stories to tell of this kind of working together for the common good at the community level. To listen to these stories from the poor themselves can be tremendously uplifting. It is one of the privileges of working in the development profession, as a promoter of participation, to see people's lives changed and improved through small-scale projects. The content of the project might be livestock improvement or water systems or community health committees. What is done is not as important as how it is done. To see successful participatory development is to see the powerless girding themselves with strength.

I wrote the following reflection after a project visit in Honduras in 1986:

On a visit to a cooperative of rural people in Honduras, the *campesinos* (literally the people of the land) told us of how they had "recuperated" some land that was not being used by a rich landlord. Here we were hearing a story of liberation through the efforts of the poor themselves, taking their destiny into their own hands, and at some risk to themselves. We were moved to see how much the donation from Heifer Project of a few head of cattle meant to them. These cows represented a hope for the future far beyond the material value of the dollars that had been sent. It was a gift of life. It meant solidarity.

There appear to be several pillars necessary for effectiveness in promoting participatory human development: solidarity, critical awareness of "reality," and a desire to work together for a fair and equitable life. Latin American indigenous groups use the term *reivindicación*, which carries with it the flavor of "claiming our rights."

The pillars of participatory development ultimately depend on the people themselves, not on outside helping agents. The role of the outsider, the helper, is to accompany the community on the road that the people themselves decide to take. More will be said about how this is done in another section of this book. Suffice it to say here that there are many potholes in that road and detours are easily taken.

A CASE FROM CHILE

In 1973, the Chilean military under General Augusto Pinochet seized power from the elected government of Salvador Allende. The generals ran the country as a virtual dictatorship for the next sixteen years. During this time the people were denied many basic human rights, and it was difficult and dangerous to organize as grassroots communities. Unions, student organizations, and political parties were banned or closely watched. It was a time when people found hope and strength in the solidarity of their grassroots organizations. During those years, many NGOs and churches supported development projects in an attempt to keep the spark of hope alive.

I have been impressed with a church-related health program in Chile that started small and grew as a team effort of women who were committed to participation and social justice. Karen Anderson, a health professional who works in Chile as a missioner of the Evangelical Lutheran Church in America, described the process she has accompanied for more then a decade in a program called EPES, *Educación Popular en Salud* (Popular Health Education). Remember that the word *popular* in Latin America means something that is of the people. The goal of this program, a ministry of the Lutheran Church in Chile, is to improve the health of the poor by helping the people organize themselves.

> Sonia and Elvira were trained as health promoters four years ago. As committed members of a local health team, their major goal is health education. It's a frustrating job. Many of the church programs in the settlement are paternalistic, and just encourage people to accept their misery, according to Elvira. She thinks God is on the side of the poor, and thinks the church should be too — not by giving handouts, but by helping people to organize and confront the injustices they face.
>
> Today Sonia's cramped two-room home is filled with newsprint, felt-tip markers and health flyers. Sonia and Elvira are preparing a class on nutrition for women who work in a local soup kitchen. Although they know it will take a lot more than a workshop on nutrition to end hunger, they hope to help the women make the best use of the few resources they have.
>
> Primary health care must go beyond teaching people about the four food groups to analyzing and confronting the root causes of ill-health. It must encourage people to take more control over their own health, lives, communities and nations....

The ministry of EPES works for "health for all" by standing in solidarity with the poor in their struggle for a more just world. There are no easy answers to resolve the overwhelming health problems, hardships and suffering of the poor. But the witness, strength and courage of the Sonias and Elviras challenge the church to join them in their struggle.[4]

In my career in development I have known many people who are working for a better tomorrow for themselves and for their families, communities, and countries. Many of them are among the poorest of the poor. I would affirm what Patrick Breslin writes about development and dignity:

And what they had in common, every one, was dignity. I became convinced that no matter how abysmal the economic level, how desperate the need for assistance, there is no point at which the dignity of the person is not more important than the aid itself.[5]

LIMITATIONS OF THE PARTICIPATORY APPROACH

While the strength of the participatory approach arises from collective action and solidarity, the cause of many failures arises from some very common human characteristics. Egoism, apathy, greed, the desire to get ahead at the cost of others are all negative influences and obstacles to participatory development. These characteristics are not found only among the poor, of course.

In all cultures, the lack of common and shared vision is a frequent malady of many organizations, including churches, industries, voluntary organizations, and governments. Conflicts and lack of a cooperative spirit are found among the rich and the poor alike. However, when such attitudes are prevalent among the poor, they can be obstacles to their own progress and moreover, can be used by dominant interests and the powerful to manipulate and divide people's organizations.

Some examples of failures that I have seen in development projects are the following:

- A workshop set up in Chile with the enthusiastic participation of a group of women to produce clothes, embroidery, and other crafts had to shut down because of a lack of market. Though participation and solidarity were high in the beginning, the project had unrealistic goals and assumptions about working in a highly competitive capitalistic society. Enthusiasm gave way to disappointment.

- A program that developed and introduced "appropriate technology" to rural subsistence farmers in the high plateau of Bolivia was evaluated and found to be using technology that was too expensive and actually inappropriate for the *campesinos*. Good intentions and the desire to help on the part of the technicians were not a sufficient substitute for the difficult and tedious work of organization and consciousness raising that might have led to a different type of project if the people had defined it themselves.

- Hand-operated water pumps were provided to communities in Honduras that organized a water committee and promised to contribute the labor to dig the wells. Dozens of water wells were dug and pumps were installed. However, after the initial work was completed and the pumps started to present maintenance problems, the communities were not sufficiently prepared to repair them and continue to administer the wells as a community enterprise. This was a technical problem, but more crucially, an organizational and management problem.

DOES IT WORK?

All agencies that sponsor and support development projects in marginated communities claim that they are getting results and that their particular approach does help the people for which their assistance is intended. If they did not believe that they would have a hard time continuing to function and raising the necessary funds to do so from their constituency.

My observation is that there are many successful examples of participatory development, and I have high regard for most private development organizations. Nevertheless, much more research and evaluation needs to be done. Participatory development is not easy, and not always successful.

The Inter-American Foundation, a government agency that supports many development projects with grassroots organizations in Latin America and the Caribbean, promotes the participatory approach. IAF has done a better job of documenting development projects than have most international assistance agencies. In the introduction to a book of case studies of such projects, the editors say this about the question of whether or not grassroots development works:

> Certainly, grassroots development is not presented here as a magic solution to the problem of poverty. The book does not conclude that self-help is a substitute for just and competent governments or efficient, effective, and equitable macroeconomic policies. Self-help cannot by itself replace large-scale development projects and programs. And it does not always succeed, or at least not readily.[6]

Chapter Seven

RELIEF, DEVELOPMENT, AND WHAT ELSE?

In Search of Transformation

> An atheist is someone who fails to practice justice
> toward the poor. If I am hungry, that is a material prob-
> lem; I need bread to eat. But if I know someone who
> is hungry it is a spiritual problem.
>
> —Anonymous

Development professionals have long had difficulty coming
up with a concise and meaningful definition of development.
In North America the idea of development is usually associated with economic growth, and numerous aid programs
are directed to this goal. However, there are many critics of
an approach to development that sees the answer to human
aspirations primarily in terms of the creation of wealth and
material accumulation.

Transformation is both a material and a spiritual challenge. The term "transformation" is increasingly being used
in some sectors as a concept that goes beyond the material and social understanding of human development. It
also considers spiritual, moral, and value aspects of change.
Transformation calls for changes in the individual (you and
me) as well as in the institutions and structures of society in which we live (us). It is about equity, which at its

heart is very biblical: "It is a question of equality.... At the moment your surplus meets their need, but one day your need may be met from their surplus. The aim is equality; as Scripture has it, 'The man who got much had no more than enough, and the man who got little did not go short'" (2 Cor. 8:14–15).

If we use the "teach them to fish" imagery, we would have to stretch our analogy far beyond merely teaching the poor to fish. Here we are more concerned with justice. What is needed would be fair and adequate credit to buy the fishing pole, an uncontaminated river, and a fair price and secure market for the catch. Perhaps underlying it all would be the assurance of the rights of everyone along the riverbank to fish.

The goal of transformational human promotion is the creation of new and just social relationships. Whereas assistance, teaching, and development projects tend to be something the rich part of the world tries to do *for* and *with* the poor part of the world, transformation is equally as necessary in the "developed" as in the "underdeveloped" world.

The concept of transformation has much to do with human values and the changes that are required in order to make a transition to personal and corporate responsibility in an increasingly fragile and interconnected world. David Korten asserts that "the priority of the current decade must be the transformation of our values, technology and institutions — in both North and South — as a prelude to setting a new pattern for the restoration of growth consistent with justice, sustainability and inclusiveness. Transformation, not growth, defines the essential global development priority for the 1990s and the only path to resolving the crisis."[1]

Jim DeVries of Heifer Project argues for a holistic model of change. He says that transformation is a cyclical model, not a straight linear process suggested in most development models:

The transformation model differs significantly from the traditional development model. It is much more than a model for bringing about economic change or trans- ferring technology. It adds the spiritual and value dimensions which are commonly ignored in develop- ment planning.[2]

DeVries goes on to point out that this model does not argue for spiritual change as more important than other as- pects. Rather, a holistic view of people and change suggests that all parts are important because all interrelate.[3]

THE CRY FOR JUSTICE

Then I looked again at all the injustice that goes on in this world. The oppressed were crying, and no one would help them. No one would help them because their oppressors had power on their side.

—Ecclesiastes 4:1

How do those who are creatively searching for transforma- tion understand the poor? Who are the poor and why are there so many of them? Simply put the poor are victims of unjust structures. They are the oppressed. And if there are oppressed people it is because there are also oppressors.

Many theologians and other scholars have identified in- justice as intimately related to poverty. "Unjust relationships and power structures need to be transformed into just ones, eliminating privileges for the few that are bought at the cost of the many." Wayne Bragg makes this point and quotes from an encyclical by Pope Paul VI.[4]

A just vision of the transformed world is: where every man, no matter what his race, religion or nationality, can live a fully human life, freed from servitude im- posed on him by other men or national forces over which he has no control (*Populorum Progressio*, 1967).

WORKING AT TRANSFORMATION

We build the road and the road builds us.[5]

One great practitioner of transformation in modern times was Martin Luther King, Jr. He challenged the mentality of structured and ingrained racism and inspired transformation of both attitudes and the legal apparatus in the United States. King wrote: "We are called to play the Good Samaritan on life's roadside; but that will only be an initial act. One day we must see that the whole Jericho road must be *transformed* so that men and women will not be constantly beaten and robbed as they make their journey on life's highway."[6]

Transformation can be a complex and slow process or one of rapid change. When we are in the middle of it we often can see only small signs of change, not the full-blown and complete achievement of solutions to human problems. Transformation is most notable where small actions turn into larger people's movements that gain momentum for changing unjust conditions. Consider the following example from Brazil:

"The church does not foment social conflicts nor provoke confrontation with the regime. The struggles are going on and the church puts itself on the side of the people." These are the words of Werner Fuchs, pastor of the Evangelical Lutheran Church (of Brazil), and one of the leaders of the movement of six thousand people who had their land expropriated because of the construction of a hydroelectric plant at Itaipu.

Representatives of the Pastoral Commission on Land and the Justice and Peace Commission met with workers and labor leaders to discuss the problems related to the possession of lands and expropriations that have been carried out by the hydroelectric company.

"The people and the church are united in this concern, and this tie is stronger than any threat," says the pastor. Thanks to dialogue and the popular protest movements, the people were able to help get the Prov-

incial (legislative assembly) to readjust the price paid
to the people for their expropriated land to be more in
line with the going market value.[7]

WOMEN IN DEVELOPMENT AND TRANSFORMATION

Several years ago Heifer Project International sponsored a
worldwide conference for women working in livestock development. Everyone had a good time with the acronym for
the conference: WILD (Women in Livestock Development).
It was said that "there were a lot of wild women at that
conference."

While the title was intended to catch attention and draw
a few laughs, the intent of the conference was very serious.
It was one way HPI could highlight the important role of
women in agriculture and livestock development all over the
world.

Women contribute more than half of the agricultural
work force in many areas of the world, especially in Africa.
As an important United Nations document stated, "It is now
becoming clear that a factor contributing to Africa's acute
food shortages is the way women have been systematically
excluded from access to land and from control of modern
agriculture."[8]

THE LAND ISSUE

Land is one of the biggest social justice issues in Latin America, as well as a serious ecological issue. The devastation
of the Amazon rain forest region is now well known to
the world. As large companies, government infrastructure
projects, and settlers move into the Amazon, the indigenous
people are simply moved aside and disposed of as obstacles
to "progress." In response the native peoples of these areas
have organized to defend their rights, especially the right
to their way of life, culture, and land. In turn, local private

development organizations support the efforts of the indigenous to defend their land and culture by bringing the real situation to public attention, lobbying the government for just policies, and providing legal aid to resolve land disputes. This is the work of transformation.

In Ecuador the indigenous people of both the Andean highlands and the Amazonian lowlands have become increasingly aware of the need to organize and demand that the dominant structures of the country take them into account. With increased public attention to the events leading up to the commemoration of the 1992 quincentennial (the so-called discovery of the Americas by Columbus), indigenous people began to reflect on their position in society after five hundred years of domination and exploitation. The Confederation of Indian Nations of Ecuador (CONAIE) got the attention of the government and the whole Ecuadoran population through the organization of what they refer to as the "Indian uprisings," well-planned and coordinated demonstrations, work stoppages, and closures of highways throughout the country.

In Ecuador, the Episcopal Conference of the Catholic Church played a mediating role, sitting down with representatives of people's movements and the government to dialogue about possible solutions and compromises to the demands of the indigenous people. Though CONAIE did not achieve all the goals it brought to the table, progress has been made on bringing an agenda set by the Indian people themselves to a round table with the government.

In explosive situations such as these, there is always the danger of violence. However, in Ecuador there has been a general consciousness of the wisdom of active nonviolence to raise public awareness and gain wider support. In some countries the conditions for nonviolent change are better than in others. It can be the vehicle to transform leaders of the church, politicians, the press, and the citizenry in general to the need for pro-active involvement.

HELPING: A MIXED BAG

Our experience as servants of the church with Vietnam
Christian Service during the Vietnam War took place in the
midst of intense political and military conflict. We went to
Vietnam to give aid to those most affected by the immense
destruction and dehumanization caused by war. Our activities were mostly along the lines of "assistance," but we
became acutely aware that to address human needs at their
core we were called to both bind up wounds and confront
the root causes of the conflict. In this vein a Mennonite
colleague reflected:

> We gave out food and blankets; we served in hospi-
> tals and public health clinics; we plowed unexploded
> grenades out of farmers' fields; but the more we did
> of this direct service, the more we knew we had
> to work to stop the curse of the war itself. Hence,
> we felt compelled to write, to speak, to advocate,
> to amplify the unheard voices of the victims in the
> halls of government and among the peoples of the
> nations.[9]

Vietnam as well as the Central American and African conflicts of the 1980s have compelled people of faith to look
more deeply at the issue of conflict. Church-related agencies are facing the reality that aid must be coupled with the
work of reconciliation.

A Lutheran World Relief issue paper on the subject of
conflict resolution recognizes that LWR's effectiveness as an
agency is increasingly undercut by the reality and impact
of conflict and strife on the populations with which LWR
works. "Yet seeking to be an agent of reconciliation...seems
an extraordinary undertaking — in some ways a diversion
from LWR's bread-and-butter work — development — rather
than an integral part of LWR's life."[10] This implies, as always, decisions on the use of limited resources and choices
regarding the vision for an organization's future.

PUBLIC POLICY

Our dialogue with Latin American colleagues constantly
touches the subject of the importance of informing, educating, and advocating for change in our own society. I
have heard this plea in many circumstances, particularly in
Central America, because of the strong intervention of the
United States in that region. The issues vary from country to
country, but the central point is the same. We are living in
an interconnected world in which our government's policies
and our way of life in the North profoundly affect people
in places far from our boundaries.

Lutheran World Relief and Church World Service do
some of their most important work through their jointly
supported office for public policy in Washington, D.C. Some
might wonder what the connection is between helping the
poor and politics. How do we help the poor by advocacy in
the nation's capitol?

The truth is, of course, that politics is the arena where
priorities are set for the country on the relative importance of military and social expenditures, health care, foreign
policy, and aid to other countries. It is where the big decisions are made on how tax dollars are spent. Each year
the world spends more on weapons research then on the
combined spending on developing new energy technologies,
improving human health, raising agricultural productivity,
and controlling pollution,[11] and the United States is a big
player in this international arena. Even more importantly,
U.S foreign policy on international debt, trade, and relations
between nations directly affects millions of people in poor
countries who have little voice or power.

Larry Minear, highly respected in Washington for his
work on behalf of the poor through advocacy on public
policy, feels that

> participating in the process of establishing justice and
> protecting the poor is a central expression of our Chris-
> tian faith, not a tangent or afterthought. Politics and

the political, therefore, concern the choices we make throughout our lives, as well as our stewardship of power at every level — from superpower and national to local and individual.[12]

Powerful nations like the U.S set foreign policies on the basis of perceived self-interest. Inevitably, the giving of humanitarian and development assistance to low-income nations is influenced by considerations of national interest. In the familiar example, giving people a fish reduces the vulnerability of the hungry, at least for awhile. Teaching people to fish helps some people take more control of their lives; helping people to protect their fishing rights is equipping them to live with dignity and with more equity and security about their futures. It takes enlightened politicians to act out of both national interest considerations and compassion for the interests of the hungry.

LIMITATIONS AND POSSIBILITIES
OF TRANSFORMATION

Today there are numerous causes, needs, unjust situations, and problems in the world with which we could become involved. Involvement in even a few of the critical issues of our day can burn out well-intentioned individuals. We clearly need to choose what causes we will support and set priorities.

Boards and staffs of institutions have the same problem, especially as some of them begin to reassess their roles and programs within the historical context in which they find themselves in the 1990s. Leadership of forward-looking organizations need to rethink the assumptions upon which they operate, asking questions such as: Are we to do business as usual, even with shrinking resources and greater demands for our help? Is our role basically that of assistance, education, support of development projects, or transformation? Should we be developing the capacity to function as a catalyst for some special and unique role as an agency?

One of the obvious difficulties with transformational human promotion is its nebulous nature. Consider, for example, the indicators one could use to evaluate the various approaches to human promotion.

In assistance programs one can record the amount of relief supplies delivered and the number of people who benefited from this aid. In the teaching approach the key questions are how many people learned which skills and how are they applying what was learned. Participatory development programs evaluate achievements by looking at the strength of an organization and the degree of ongoing benefits, such as improved health, nutrition, or production that the participants (communities) are enjoying.

When we turn our attention to transformation we cannot so easily evaluate measurable change. Note some of the terminology used by those who talk about transformation. How much more difficult it is to evaluate "raised consciousness," "liberation," "social movements," "changes in attitudes," "energizing networks," "critical mass of public opinion," "vision of alternative futures," and "just social relationships." Jim DeVries points out that "this model suggests areas of impact or change commonly ignored by the more quantitative, readily measurable, material, change based models."[13]

Though the goals of transformation, i.e., just social and economic relationships, are difficult to evaluate, the reality of today's world compels us to stretch our imaginations and develop new concepts of how best to engage ourselves in human promotion. It is likely that we should not choose between either/or, but engage in both/and...relief, development, and transformation.

Organizations that were originally founded to carry out relief programs and later moved to support self-help projects are now confronting a more complex and interconnected world in which the demands for their attention are many and the resources few.

Below are several criteria that may be helpful in thinking through our personal and institutional involvement in human promotion, especially if transformation is our agenda.[14] Activities, programs, and organizations in which we participate and to which we give our support should

- have a strong commitment to social justice and sustainable development as fundamental goals;

- have a theory and understanding of the root causes of the problems about which we are concerned and use some of our resources to confront these causes;

- have a participatory structure and put value on both professionalism and volunteerism, continuously striving for renewal of commitment and vision;

- actively promote voluntary participation of its constituency, not only through financial contributions, but also as a potential force for change at home and abroad.

- collaborate with other organizations and coordinate with people's movements in addressing problems of mutual concern.

Chapter Eight

SOME OFTEN-ASKED QUESTIONS

When I speak to groups about the work of church agencies in poor areas of the world, I find the question-and-answer period to be very enlightening. It is a good indicator of the interest and understanding people have about poverty, aid, and global issues. Some questions are predictable and are asked in almost every session; obviously these are issues that are on the minds of many people. The following are some questions that are often asked by people in churches and community groups. The responses to these questions are mine, except in those instances noted below.

Does the Aid Actually Get to the People Who Need It?

In my opinion church-related agencies have a substantially better chance of getting the aid to people in need than most large government programs. The principal reasons for this are two: the trusting relationship with high-quality local partner organizations and the grassroots nature of the projects. The fact that the people in these organizations are close to the scene and know the needs lends itself to close monitoring and channeling of the assistance to the neediest communities. As stated by an LWR staff person, "Because our working partners come from the communities themselves, there is less risk of our support...being diverted into inappropriate channels."

Of course, we would not be honest if we claimed that there is never diversion of resources or inefficiency in church-related organizations. Nevertheless, over many years of work with hundreds of local NGOs all over Latin America, I can only think of a few where corruption or incompetency was obvious. By and large the record of stewardship and dedication of the staff of both the donor agencies and the local partners is outstanding.

What about Politics and Repressive Governments?

Private agencies work almost exclusively with local NGOs and, thus, do not normally support or overtly side with particular policies of governments. Aid agencies almost never set out to be "political." However, international aid agencies do need to sign working agreements with governments and abide by the laws of the host country. If that government is repressive and abusive to its own citizens, what should be the stance and action of the aid agency? Being critical of human rights abuses, for example, can be risky, even life-threatening in some cases. Many have taken a stand on the side of the poor and oppressed and paid the supreme price.

There have been some ironic circumstances in respect to this question over the years. For example, why did Haiti, which for decades was one of the most repressive governments in the world, receive so much attention from international aid agencies, both private and governmental? Of course the obvious answer is the great need and poverty. However, while the majority of international agencies, many of them church-related, provided relief and service to the poor, few of them spoke out for justice and against repression during the Duvalier dictatorship. The fact is that the straightforward act of providing relief can be political and in this case may have unwittingly been supportive of a repressive government.

On the other hand, there are many examples of courageous action on the part of aid personnel and agencies. My opinion is that the most appropriate stance is to support local churches and groups that are dealing with problems and issues of justice in their own countries while at the same time advocating just policies with our own governments.

One good way to do that is to support both your favorite relief and development agency as well as Bread for the World, the Christian citizens' advocacy organization.

Can Donations Be Designated?

Every organization has its own policy on this. Most relief and development organizations encourage donors to give undesignated gifts. This allows for the broadest use of funds to meet the needs of the agency's program. Appeals for funds, therefore, allow donors to give toward the greatest need.

Nevertheless, donors often like to identify with a specific project or country. I think it is a good policy to allow for designated giving, though it should be recognized that there are drawbacks if churches and other donors relate directly to the field. Confusion, paternalism, and duplication can result.

My advice is to discuss designated giving with the organization you wish to support to find out what kind of approach is in the best interests of the people who benefit from the program.

Is the Aid Given to Christians?
Does Your Program Help to Spread the Gospel?

The staff of Heifer Project International answered this question in a way that I think is representative of the approach of many church-related relief and development programs. I would agree with the spirit of this answer:

> HPI does not discriminate on the basis of religion, race or belief. We believe that all people are children of God. Although many of the projects we fund are associated with Christian churches, this is not a criterion to receive funding. HPI has project participants who are Moslem, Buddhist, Hindu, Animist, Christian, etc. We do not ask people to change their religious belief in order to be assisted by HPI. However, our work as a Christian agency is a clear testimony of our concern and our faith.[1]

What about Child Sponsorship Programs?

Frankly, I am not positive about them. In child sponsorship programs donations are made on a regular basis to an organization for the support of a specific child in a particular country. This approach is enormously appealing because it is presented as a direct way to alleviate the poverty of at least one person in what seems like a sea of misery that begs at least some response from well-meaning people. The sponsor feels, no doubt, that the needs are overwhelming, but "at least I can do something."

In fact, while some relief and development agencies have suffered cutbacks and reduced income, child sponsorship programs have continued to prosper. It has been a growth industry for some years, and certainly the agencies that promote this approach have been successful in marketing their product, the needy child. I encourage people interested in sponsoring a child to ask the agency what their overhead is. How much of the monthly contribution is used in administration and fund raising? In addition to the question of overhead cost, the following is a synopsis of opinions I have gleaned from direct observation and from colleagues in Latin America.

Child sponsorship schemes have become a much-debated issue among relief and development professionals. Some think of it as an ethical issue for several reasons. First, there is the question of whether or not poverty and misery — the pathetic-looking child with a distended belly staring at you out of an ad or television commercial — should be "marketed." Some spokespersons from low-income countries see this as a fund-raising gimmick based on pity for the poor, something they see as contrary to promoting dignity. Some development professionals have called the fund-raising approach that uses tear-jerking pictures of starving children "pornography of the poor."

Second, many local NGOs in the Two-Thirds World are very critical of the individualistic approach that channels a steady stream of money into poor communities. They see development as a long-term process of collective action. It is felt that sponsoring selected children and channeling money to their families tends to rupture and divide communities. This is particularly harmful where the sponsorship program gives aid to families on the basis of church affiliation.

My observation is that there is practically no coordination between child sponsorship agencies and local NGOs. Indeed, there is often evidence of animosity where local NGOs and international sponsorship programs work in the same communities with differing development approaches.

Even where the sum total of all sponsorship donations is pooled to pay for community projects, which is an approach now used by several of these agencies, the criticism is still made that the agency is pushing its "packaged program." Outside resources coming on a monthly basis are not always helpful or even needed for appropriate development to take place at the pace of the local community. In fact, some colleagues in Latin America feel it is harmful. It is certainly an issue in need of both deeper understanding on the part of donors and more dialogue within NGO communities.

What Opportunities Are There for a Career in International Development?

International development work is not a growth industry in terms of job opportunities. However, it is a very interesting professional field, and there are many good organizations that offer possibilities. As in other fields, getting that first experience is crucial.[2]

When my contemporaries and I started to work in this field, there were few opportunities to study development as a profession. We had to learn from direct experience, or at least I did. Today there are opportunities to study development, but getting started and acquiring field experience may be increasingly difficult for residents of developed countries.

The message we are now receiving from many colleagues in the Two-Thirds World is that the doing of development work, especially at the grassroots, should be in the hands of professionals and promoters from the southern countries. Those of us from northern-based NGOs, churches, and other private groups should have different functions and roles.

On the one hand, the number of people who want to go to where the poor are and work directly with them is relatively small. On the other hand, the number of people within our North American and European countries who are concerned and motivated enough to want to do something about the terrible mess our world is in is relatively large. Within both categories are people who are highly motivated, sensitive, and well intentioned.

Church-related agencies do have a few overseas positions. Some hire very few (like LWR), and others offer more opportunities (such as Catholic Relief Services).[3] Though it may not be easy to break into the field, one way to get experience is to start as a volunteer.

What about Volunteer Programs? What Opportunities Are There to Go Overseas as a Volunteer?

Service as a volunteer is an excellent way to gain valuable experience, but it should be kept in mind that the greatest benefit may be to the volunteer rather than the people he or she serves. Anyone who wants to help poor people through development programs has to start somewhere to gain experience. Only through experience can one grow in maturity and acquire the skills needed to work in cross-cultural settings in programs of human development. One always makes mistakes along the way, but, hopefully, one also learns and grows in understanding and sensitivity.

Years ago I decided to make a vocational commitment and spend my life in solidarity with the poor. I've lived the last seventeen years in Fecunda de Vela, an isolated rural community about three hours off the main road in the mountains of Ecuador. Right now I'm working with a group of women who are making their living from processing and selling marmalade in the markets of Quito.

The above words are from a conversation with Carla, a volunteer from an Italian organization that supports work with rural communities in Ecuador. What Carla was telling me was challenging my assumptions about the appropriate role of outsiders in programs that aim to help the poor. Over the years I have become alternatively skeptical and enthusiastic about the real contributions that expatriates (outsiders) can make by working directly with the poor in the Two-Thirds World. Carla is, in fact, an exception. I have never known someone who has volunteered as long as Carla — she seems to have practically made a career out of it. She represents continuity, an understanding of the "reality," and a commitment to "accompaniment" over the long haul. Yet, is a long-term presence within a community a good thing? Commitment and solidarity are the positives; the creation of dependency and not letting go or "turning it over" might be negatives.

While espousing the importance of understanding development and transformation as a process, in fact, many development agencies from the North get impatient with the lack of concrete results that this slow process entails.

Most development programs, including those which deploy volunteers, have both successes and failures in their history. Some volunteers, though not all, have often come up short on long-term commitment. Even a short-term commitment is sometimes problematic. It is not unusual to find relatively high dropout rates in Peace Corps programs, for example, where the terms of service are only two years. My opinion is that a volunteer's term of service should be, at the minimum, two years, preferably three.

One of the best church-related volunteer sending organizations I have encountered is the Mennonite Central Committee (MCC). MCC provides opportunity for committed people to work in areas of poverty in many countries of the world as well as the United States. Volunteers come not only from Mennonite churches but from many other Christian denominations. Emphasis is put on Christian motivation, and one of the requisites for service is a commitment based on a statement of faith.[4]

Besides the service rendered in numerous areas of need, including war zones, the MCC volunteer program has contributed in a major way to the Mennonite Church's high level of social awareness, service, and support of mission in their home countries. Mennonite churches often have a much greater per member record of giving to missions than other denominations. Mennonite volunteer programs challenge people to become involved in social service, justice, and peace in very direct ways. It is an outlet for service and identification with the poor that seems lacking in many other denominations.

Lutheran World Relief no longer has a volunteer program. It discountinued this activity in the late 1980s. The experience raised many questions and challenges for LWR, including the realization that a quality volunteer program requires a high level of organization, good support systems, and funding.

Today, if a person asks what the options are for working with a volunteer program, I usually refer him or her to MCC if it is a person who is interested in working with the church. The other avenue is the Peace Corps in which thousands of people have gained experience and exposure to the issues and needs of the Two-Thirds World. Nevertheless, it is commonly said by people who have served as volunteers that the greatest value was the learning experience they themselves gained. So much the better if, coincidentally, they were also able to make a contribution for the good of the people with whom they lived and worked.[5]

I've Heard That Food Rots on the Docks

Fortunately, most agencies have not had to face this problem. By tight management on the spot, good communications, and working with efficient partner agencies rather than with governments, food spoilage has been largely avoided.

However, some reports you may have heard about food rotting on the docks are accurate. This is usually due to war conditions, poor transport systems, and inadequate harbor facilities. Famine in our time is often linked to wars and unrest. Moreover, these famines take place in countries with very scarce resources such as paved roads, functioning harbors, cranes to unload food, and enclosed warehouses to store food. Also in war situations many things can happen to worsen these problems.

American agencies work with local relief and development organizations who know the situation on the ground. Despite this, there is some loss of food, though it is minimal. All precautions are taken to minimize the loss of precious food and agencies are proud of their overall record on this account.

Why Should We Help People Who Keep Having Large Families?

Many factors enter into the equation of whether people will have large families. An obvious one is lack of access to birth control. In India, for example, 22 percent of the women would like to limit the size of their families but have no access to contraception materials. In Egypt, the figure is 26 percent; in Peru it is 45 percent. Supplies to remote villages, where the majority of people live, are unreliable.

Another factor in enabling people to limit the size of their families is related to cultural values. In many countries a man may refuse to allow his wife to use contraception. In these cultures, a man's worth is measured by the number of children his wife bears.

In some countries families actively choose to have many children with the sad knowledge that only a portion of them will make it to adulthood. In rural societies where you eat what you grow or what others give you, a child is often the only form of social security.

But perhaps the most important factor in family size is the status of women. Often a woman's only option to gain status is through motherhood.

To address all these factors that tend to make people have large families we need to ensure families that their children will survive by supporting prenatal and maternal health care. And we can help women to have fewer children by supporting efforts to increase their stature in society and through education and access to birth control.

How Do Agencies Select the Groups to Work With?

In development work, the people for whom the projects are initiated are involved from the very beginning. It does no good in the long term for an agency to arrive on the scene, study the situation, and then proceed to solve the problems without the participation of the people involved. A well drilled or a health-care worker trained may be of benefit for a while, but in the absence of a felt need and project participation, the benefits will inevitably fall into disuse.

Also, choices for projects are made on the basis of limited resources. Agencies must choose to concentrate on areas with the greatest suffering. This means, for example, that in Latin America we concentrate on Peru, Bolivia, and Ecuador rather than on Uruguay or Argentina, where the needs and suffering are not as great. In all cases, also, agencies try not to duplicate work being done by other agencies and often support the relief work done by others in these areas.

What Do Development Agencies Do in the Area of Helping Women?

Agencies do recognize the key role of women in development and also the fact that women are often disproportionately represented among the poor and oppressed.

Some projects focus exclusively on women. One example is a project in ten villages in West Africa where carefully trained female health workers integrate themselves into the communities so that an atmosphere of trust, respect, and empathy is established. Projects in other places include components that address women's needs in a broader context such as literacy classes and other training that help women to learn skills that they can use to enhance their standing in their families and communities. The goal of increased opportunities and more equitable standing for women is a part of the program of all agencies working in development.

Part III

TOWARD A PRACTICE OF ACCOMPANIMENT

In the decade of the 1990s much is being written about the challenges of world poverty and massive environmental degradation facing the world. Special attention is being focused on the role of nongovernmental organizations (NGOs), people's movements, and churches as alternatives that offer a degree of hope in what often seems like a world of overwhelming needs and problems.

Current thinking is that people involved in voluntary action will take on increasing importance in achieving equitable development due to their flexibility to respond to changing environments. Voluntary organizations have greater ability to work creatively with people at the grassroots than governments.

During the 1980s and into the 1990s Lutheran World Relief has been trying to do just that, working at what it calls the "accompaniment" approach to development cooperation in the Andean region. In this region LWR's program of development cooperation has been underway since 1979 through the work of its Andean Regional Office (ARO). It is certainly germane for us to look back over more than a decade of attempts to forge partnerships with local nongovernmental organizations in the counties of Peru, Ecuador, Bolivia, and Chile.

A word about terminology is in order. The historical relationship between a local NGO and an international organization, such as LWR, was based on the "donor-recipient" model. In this relationship the local NGO is sometimes a mere intermediary that implements projects. In some cases, the international agency would prefer to bypass the intermediary and work directly in the project area. Heavy shades of paternalism and inequality permeate this relationship.

The term "partnership" has been put forth to describe an ideal relationship, never perfectly realized, between the international agency and the local NGO. The fact that it is only partially achieved does not diminish its importance. Because it is an ideal it must be continually worked on. But wait, says the astute observer, what about the people in the communities who are said to be the primary actors in development? Participation in the development process, after all, refers to the local people, not to development professionals and/or volunteers from the outside.

This is where partnership gets more complex. The partnership model is, as Mario Padrón put it, a "three partners" relationship. The three partners are (1) the grassroots organization, (2) the local NGO, and (3) the international institution for development cooperation.[1] Each of these organizations works together on a common area of concern (usually a project), but each retains autonomy and relationships beyond the project. Partnership is not a marriage, nor is it a stringent business contract. It is a relationship based upon trust and shared objectives.

Let me emphasize that the ideal in this partnership should be the inverse of what it usually is in the real world. The people in grassroots organizations in the Two-Thirds World should be seen as the most important of the three partners, holding their "junior partners," the NGOs and funding agencies, accountable for their actions. The grassroots organizations mobilize their own resources, the people, their organizational capability, and their experience. They have numbers (they are not wealthy but they are many), know-how, traditional values of solidarity, and traditions of mutual help, and they have their own concrete solutions for problems.[2]

It is in the context of striving to attain this dynamic three-way partnership that LWR has been working on a methodology of accompaniment in the Andean region. In this section I attempt to describe this method.

INSTITUTIONAL LEARNING

LWR, as well as many other organizations that work with the poor, has been going through a time of reflection and transition. A serious effort has been made to evaluate achievements and document learnings from past experience.

Learning from experience is important, even though sometimes the effort leads to more questions than answers. Numerous internal discussions, evaluations, stories, and other documents have been written in an attempt to describe to ourselves and others what the accompaniment experiment has meant and what has been achieved through it.

Some of the questions we have asked ourselves are these: What has been learned from the accompaniment approach used by LWR during these years? Is there something here that should be shared with our colleagues in the development community as well as with our faithful supporters in the churches? Can we describe in succinct terms the measurable benefits of our work and methodology?

GIVING OUR APPROACH A NAME

One of the most intriguing titles I have run into for a church-related assistance organization was a center in El Salvador related to the Baptist Church. It was called Ser con mi Hermano — which means (excuse the exclusive language) "Being with my Brother." "With" is a powerfully symbolic word and conjures up in our minds the idea of presence, nearness, and being in the company of another. It is at the core of what we mean by accompaniment.

LWR's work in the Andean region of South America has attempted to build on the spirit and concept of previous LWR efforts in other parts of the world, the idea of "being with."

The following presentation encompasses three broad aspects of the work of human development based on the ideal of partnership. First of all, it is critical in the accompaniment approach to consider the social, cultural, and historical context of the country and people with whom we work. Secondly, the day-to-day work of accompaniment takes place through human relationships working in concrete programs. Finally, accompaniment is based on underlying values; primary among these are mutual respect and dignity.

Chapter Nine

LATIN AMERICA
The Context

A look at some historical roots is helpful here. After more than four and a half centuries of imposing doctrines and forms of worship on the people of Latin America, the 1960s and 1970s saw churches (both Catholic and Protestant) beginning to practice respect for the cultures and beliefs of the people of Latin American countries.

Pastoral workers at both a local and hierarchical level began to explore the need to "accompany" the people in their communities in their search to discover and work out their own destiny. Much analysis was done of the dramatic levels of poverty in the countries of Latin American. People started asking, "Why does so much poverty exist?"

Some Christians began to arrive at disturbing conclusions, especially as they reflected on this reality in the light of their faith. Various pastoral documents that came out of the Latin American Catholic Church pronounced that it was time to listen to and learn from people instead of continuing to force them to assume ideas that are foreign to their cultures and condescending to them as persons.

Church-related agencies from northern countries that were in contact with Latin American churches and grass-roots leaders were forced to face the question of how North American people should relate to and think about the poor. Christians in the South challenged Christians and others in the North to think seriously about the injustice and op-

103

pression that was so rampant in Latin America and what
a proper response might be for people of conscience.

To better understand the roots of the concept of accompaniment in Latin America, it is helpful to look at some of
the roots of a theology that began to be formed within the
Latin American context during this time.

LIBERATION THEOLOGY[1]

The 1960s was an important decade for the renewal of the
Roman Catholic Church, particularly in Latin America. Three
important factors are related to this phenomenon, two of
them arising from within the church itself and one external
to the church.

As the decade began, Pope John XXIII, a great reformer of
the Catholic Church, launched a missionary challenge to the
churches of the North asking them to turn their attention
toward Latin America. Though Latin America had always
been seen as a "Catholic continent," it was now recognized
as a continent without pastors. The pope called on the rich
churches from the North to fill the void.

Bishops called for religious of the orders and dioceses to
take up this challenge and, indeed, there was a substantial
response as priests and nuns from the United States, Canada, Ireland, and mainland Europe began to head for Latin
America. This was soon to change the life of the church in
Latin America.

These pastoral agents, both lay and clergy, were highly
motivated to serve and evangelize in Latin America, but they
came with practically no understanding of what they would
encounter. Many, in fact, held to a fervent anti-communist
mentality that was common at that time in their own cultures and countries. Though they did not understand Latin
America and its people, they were giving and generous,
open to learning. They came with a strong desire to serve
the church and the people of Latin America.

This was the beginning of a conversion experience, prin-

cipally for the religious themselves, as they began to understand the depths of misery and the terrible struggle for daily
existence in the places where they had gone to "minister to
the poor."

While this had a profound effect on these servants of
God, the encounter also had a positive effect on the people in the villages and *barrios* of Latin America. For the first
time in its history the church was coming close to the poor
in Latin America. The servants of the church, who traditionally had been associated with the powerful and had been
seen as somewhat exploitative, were now in direct contact
with the masses of poor people. In many cases they lived
among the people. For the first time the poor were getting
to know a more generous and humble clergy, no longer simply the priest who came to the community once a year to
perform baptisms and marriages and to celebrate Mass, and
then charge a fee for these "services."

Later, as liberation theology developed a terminology to
talk about this phenomenon, the phrase "theology as a second act" emerged. The first act was the faith experience
of the poor themselves; the second was a reflection on
that faith experience. Liberation theology became a way of
reflecting on biblical truths out of that process.

A second factor that gave rise to liberation theology was
the impact of two historical events that took place within the
Roman Church, Vatican Council II in Rome and the Latin
American bishops' meeting in Medellín, Colombia, in 1968.
The bishops' meeting is considered to be one of the land-
mark religious as well as political events of this century. Two
key words that came to the forefront at the meeting were
"liberation" and "participation," providing the theological basis for the rise of the "base Christian community" movement
in Latin America.[2] As a result of this meeting, where some
of the concepts of liberation theology were first formally introduced by Gustavo Gutiérrez, the bishops proclaimed that
the church should make a "preferential option for the poor."

In both of these events, one of the questions posed
was "What is the place of the church?" In response, many

religious and lay people were motivated to act out their convictions by accompanying the poor and being present where they live. Moreover, some of these religious workers took the decidedly radical option of joining people's movements, unions, and community organizations in actions that were often seen by those in power as subversive and communist-inspired.

The term "accompaniment" was used in one well-known case in El Salvador where martyrdom was the result of working with the poor. Four church women were tortured and assassinated in El Salvador on December 2, 1980. Melinda Roper, president of the Maryknoll Sisters, the order to which two of the women belonged, wrote,

> Maura, Ita, Dorothy, and Jean are remembered as martyrs. The psychological, political and spiritual analyses have given way to the stark reality of four women who loved the people of El Salvador and were willing to accompany them in times of great suffering and ...because they lived as disciples of Jesus of Nazareth came face to face with the power of evil in its ultimate manifestation of violent death.... The four women were in El Salvador to accompany and walk with the poor. They were in El Salvador as members of a church that is persecuted because it is identified with the cause of the poor.[3]

A third factor related to the development of liberation theology has to do with the social and political processes that were underway in Latin America in the 1960s. A demographic explosion began to change dramatically the very nature of the urban centers of the continent. Lima, a pleasant colonial city where the oligarchy of the country lived the good life and had benefited for many generations from the historical alignment of church, state, and military, was invaded by poor people from the countryside. This "irruption of the poor" into history brought not only an increase in the number of poor people, but also demonstrated their surprising organizational capacity. In some of the most dramatic examples of this, thousands of people "invaded" lands on the outskirts of major cities to claim these spaces as new urbanization settlements. In Lima, these were called *pueblos jóvenes* (new towns).

Having read about this phenomenon, I was still not prepared for the breathtaking impact of seeing it happen in 1972. The "invasion" I observed was eventually to form the massive *pueblo joven* of Villa El Salvador in the desert outside of Lima. From one day to the next literally tens of thousands of people appeared to mark out and claim their space in the sand.

In one *pueblo joven,* Canto Grande, on the northeast side of Lima, land invasions beginning in the mid-1970s mushroomed the population and land area from a small semirural town of ten thousand to a massive slum of a half million people within a decade. The original land invasion itself was made by forty thousand people. With such a large number of people and such puissant changes compressed into a short time frame, it was necessary to think of new ways of ministry and of "being the church."

There was a great ferment and a dynamic stirring and awareness among these migrant people that challenged the traditional holders of power. In numerous instances throughout the continent militant elements took up armed struggle in an attempt to bring about radical political change. The cities simply could not absorb the floods of people and survival became the way of life for tens of thousands. Thus, Christians who sided with the poor had to debate and rationalize their stance on armed struggle as an option for the poor.

This sociopolitical factor that gave rise to liberation theology was external to the church, but very much a part of the context. Latin American sociologists and economists began to develop theories to interpret poverty. One of the most prominent of these was dependency theory, which arose in reaction to the growing disparities between rich and poor nations. Social scientists saw the root cause of underdevelopment as overdevelopment in the industrialized countries.

According to this logic, the development of a country on the periphery needs good markets for its products in the countries that are at the center of the world economic system, thus making the resource-poor country dependent on the rich country. A classic example of this is the so-called banana republics of Honduras and Guatemala.

While a theology that responds to the reality of poverty and oppression is not totally contingent on sociopolitical analysis, there was a felt need for instruments to help analyze and understand the root causes of the unjust conditions in which so many millions live in Latin America. Those who were trying to understand causes of poverty used sociological tools, including Marxist analysis, in countless documents, meetings, and projects as a way to interpret reality. Subsequently, some of the assumptions upon which this theory are based have been discarded.[4] Marxist analysis does not seem to be heard as much in meetings and discussions of development in Latin America as it previously was.

GRASSROOTS DEMOCRACY

In the 1960s and 1970s the prevalent ideology of those who held the political and economic power in most Latin American countries was the national security doctrine. This ideology allowed those in charge to hold on to their power at any cost in the name of anti-communism. In country after country, military dictatorships held power, more often than not supported by their ally from the north, Uncle Sam. Anything that seemed to threaten the status quo was considered subversive and to be repressed with force whenever it was seen as necessary or simply convenient. Thus, democracy was weak or nonexistent in much of Latin America during these decades.

However, the large peasant, labor, and urban movements gave form to grassroots political democracy in a number of Latin American countries. Although the struggle of progressive political leaders and parties was very important, it was the peasants' struggle for land, the people's struggle to organize in the cities, and the union workers' struggle to attain their rights that formed the beginnings of these still weak democracies in Latin America.

These mass organizations have gone through alternating cycles of effectiveness and ineffectiveness in their efforts to influence public policies and gain access to power at the economic and political level. They have almost always suffered from lack of resources and technical support to gain their ends.

Peasant movements that have had an important role in occupying and taking over land find that once land has been occupied or ownership of large tracts has been abolished they are at a loss to know what to do with these extensive areas of land. Faced with a lack of credit or technology, an eventual alternative is the breaking up of the movement as peasants parcel land into small holdings. The same phenomenon happens in urban movements.[5]

Thus, private sector development organizations began to work with these grassroots movements, believing that the single most important contribution to self-determination and development lies in empowerment of people through their own organizations.

THE NONGOVERNMENT SECTOR

Finally, the above factors all came together to give impetus to the rise of nongovernmental organizations (NGOs) as an alternative for the channeling of creative energies and resources to empower the poor. Most of these NGOs began as part of a church structure or as quasi-ecclesiastical organizations, though for various reasons many of them have become independent since their inception. Many highly qualified and motivated Latin American professionals and technicians began to work with these NGOs.

In addition to the quality of their teams, the NGO sector has grown tremendously in numbers in both the North and the South. Thomas Dichter estimates that 2500 northern NGOs with a Two-Thirds World focus exist in the economically developed countries (primarily Europe, Canada, and the U.S.), with tens of thousands of people on the payrolls. The number of southern NGOs that work in development in their respective countries is staggering, running into the tens of thousands. In Peru alone there are at least 450 such organizations,[6] and in Chile and Bolivia the numbers are similar.

Mario Padrón, a Peruvian development specialist, described this as an "NGO boom," which started in the 1960s and grew dramatically in the 1980s. He described how, in Peru,

> young professionals found in the NGOs and their projects an alternative to governmental schemes, the fruitless rhetorical discussions of party politics, and/or the academic isolation from the problems of their countries. . . . Several factors explain such a situation [in Latin America]: dramatic poverty levels, mobilization and organization of the poor, government efforts at modernization, availability of technicians (indigenous intelligentsia), and international development fund availability.[7]

When LWR began its work by setting up the Andean Regional Office in the late 1970s, there was already an established NGO community in each of the countries of the Andean region. Although they had a number of weaknesses, which an LWR study had detected in 1977, NGOs also had development experience that could be built upon and around which the accompaniment model was to be developed.

Chapter Ten

ACCOMPANIMENT

An Experiment
in the Andean Region

Since the early 1960s, Lutheran World Relief has provided material aid, responded to disasters, and participated in community development in several Latin American countries. During those years work was done through a limited number of ecumenical partner organizations.[1]

The major earthquake that struck Managua in 1972 provided an opportunity to begin a new phase of cooperation in Nicaragua and in Central America. Through its direct experience in subsequent years LWR evolved a clearer perception of how it wanted to confront the problems of development and assistance to people living in poverty. The agency decided to attempt to work out new forms of partnership between the North and the South through a program in the Andean region of South America.

When LWR set up the Andean Regional Office (ARO) in 1979, it resolved to take "a new approach."[2] With the decision to establish the Andean Regional Office, Hans Hoyer was contracted to work out of Lima as the first director. Hans had extensive experience in Latin America and many contacts and relationships as a result of his previous work with Catholic Relief Services.

Four objectives were set for this office, and only the last one had to do with funding of development projects in the manner of more traditional programs. The objectives of ARO can be summarized as: (1) building up the capacity of local organizations, (2) networking and making linkages between NGOs and the grassroots, (3) helping local NGOs to improve their ability to evaluate the programs, and (4) funding participatory development projects.

From the beginning, ARO "maintained a modest profile, a factor that undoubtedly contributed to its success in establishing positive and open relationships with local social action groups."[3] LWR did not want to convey a mistaken perception of its capacity for giving financial assistance. On the contrary, staff was conscious of LWR's meager resources and that ARO should not start or carry out projects by itself or be the driving force for change at the community level.

It was felt then, and still is, that there are many competent and highly motivated teams of Latin Americans who can do the work of development. They are more connected to the local context and culture than foreigners who might come in to set up their own programs, and they are often very motivated to do something for their own country and people.

WHAT IS ACCOMPANIMENT?

LWR staff has been using the term "accompaniment" to describe the methodology and philosophy of the agency's work in the Andean region. Even to ourselves this term has sometimes seemed vague and "un-scientific." The term is certainly not found in any of the literature on management, and seldom in writings in the development field. It does, however, appear in the thinking and reflections that have come out of the grassroots movements in Latin America over the last two decades, particularly since the early 1970s when a sector within the Catholic Church began to make the "preferential option for the poor" in the post-Medellín era.[4]

The philosophy of accompaniment can be seen in the flesh in various places in Latin America. It is made particularly visible when seen in the lives of the many people who have taken this option, especially priests, nuns, and volunteers who decided to live and work among the poor in the massive urban slums of the great cities of Latin America. But what does this mean when translated to programs of a relief and development agency like Lutheran World Relief? The role of a project officer, technical advisor, or consultant of an international NGO is often quite different from that of those who work more directly with the poor at the grassroots.

The staff of the Andean Regional Office (ARO) started to use the term "accompaniment" to explain its way of working with counterparts, both church-related and secular NGOs. The ARO team wanted to understand specific problems as well as the context in which they arose. The concept involves a strong commitment of solidarity in which the funding of projects is only one of the tools of international cooperation.

ARO sees accompaniment as a methodology that makes a dynamic three-way partnership, i.e., the grassroots organization, the local NGO, and LWR. One important goal of accompaniment is to help the grassroots leaders to gain confidence in themselves so they can decide what their own future is to be. In practical terms for an international agency, LWR's primary working relationship is with its partner NGOs, which, in turn, work directly with grassroots communities.

LWR'S UNDERSTANDING OF DEVELOPMENT

On the spectrum of thinking about the theory and practice of development, Lutheran World Relief comes out on the "people-centered" side of the debate. While the central thrust of development in the post–World War II period has been toward ever-increasing production and consumption, the concerns of people-centered development are human growth and well-being, equity and sustainability.[5]

There have been many attempts to define development

in literature. LWR constantly has to re-examine its assumptions and approach to its work in a world of hunger, injustice, and poverty. It is only when objectives and purpose are clear that an organization can sharpen its program of assistance to the world's poor. The term "development assistance" has been widely used over the years. Nevertheless, at the prompting of our southern partners, we have been sensitized to use the term "development cooperation" as one that gives a better sense of the relationship between partners. The late Mario Padrón of Peru, a constant friend of LWR throughout the 1980s, did much to advance the thinking and terminology of partnership between North and South and helped LWR to sharpen its own understanding of "accompaniment." Mario always challenged the northern agencies to think in terms of partnership and cooperation rather than implementing their own projects in Two-Thirds World countries.

DEVELOPMENT TERMINOLOGY

In the voluminous writings on the subject of development today, much of the terminology is quite widely accepted and commonly used by many agencies. Application in the field is a different matter, however. I have sat in seminars where development is being discussed and where practically everyone agrees on the importance of the "participation of the people themselves." Yet, when I visit communities in countries like Bolivia and Ecuador, where there are a large number of development projects carried out by a variety of agencies, I see great diversity in the way these organizations work. It is obvious that what is participation to one group is imposition and paternalism to another.

Patrick Breslin of the Inter-American Foundation said it well when he made the point that "the donor of assistance must be a true partner to the recipient. The air turns thick with the constant repetition of these lessons, but in project after project around the world they are repeatedly violated.

No one questions them, but few know how to put them into practice."[6]

1979–82: A TIME FOR LEARNING

The Andean Regional Office was set up in Lima to cover the countries of Peru, Bolivia, Ecuador, and Chile. For various reasons, including proximity to the problems and opportunities, a high proportion of the resources that LWR directed to the Andean region have gone into Peru.

ARO did not seek to address specific short-term economic needs, of which there are many in the Andean region. On the contrary, ARO sought to be available when a local NGO faced concrete needs, giving special importance to building up in them the capacity to promote community organization.

It was indispensable to really get to know the groups and the place where local teams were working, as seen in this letter from the director of ARO to one of LWR's new partners in Peru:

During the short time that I have known you, I have been very impressed with your commitment and dedication to the *campesinos* [peasants] of the Huacho area. I understand very well that the struggle for justice and social equality will not be accomplished soon....It is a struggle which will take all our lifetime and that of future generations.

Through this small contribution...we want to express our commitment of solidarity regarding your work. We are aware that our help is very limited and does not solve the economic needs of the Campesino Student Home. But we are very conscious that the solution of its problems should never come from outside. We have already seen the extraordinary capacity of the *campesinos* for finding their own solutions for resolving their problems. They should never increase their dependence on persons or institutions which do not really belong to their region. We feel very privileged to be able to "accompany" and learn more about your work.[7]

This need for direct contact was also due to the desire to feel the pulse of the country and learn more about its problems and potential. This made it possible to contact many people and grassroots organizations involved in the search for alternative solutions to their problems.

LWR's partners frequently encounter difficulties, as seen in this letter from one of them:

I hope that your work will allow you a little time to escape to Cusco after the rains, in order to go to Chincheros (actually the vehicle cannot get to the medical post, you have to wade in mud up to the knees!). The carrying out of the small hog enterprise is slow — the legal procedures for the ownership of the land have been considerably delayed. But even more lamentable is the sudden death of the young president of the production committee, due to incurable tuberculosis caused by chronic malnutrition suffered since childhood. The project has not been abandoned, nevertheless. The other members have accepted the challenge of fighting precisely against malnutrition through increasing their production.[8]

Pedro Veliz of the LWR office in Lima later reflected, "We learned that the financial assistance from LWR/ARO was not the only worthwhile contribution. Because of this fact we did not set up rigid criteria, though we still insisted on the importance of accountability."

Small micro-projects showed LWR staff that putting the projects in the hands of the people demonstrates a double trust: a trust in their knowledge of how to resolve problems, and trust in their integrity in the handling of funds.

Characteristic of this learning phase in the life of ARO, great efforts were made to facilitate small projects. LWR set up a special budget called the Andean Development Facilitation Fund (ADFF), which could be administered by the ARO director for small projects costing up to $3,000. During its first four years, ARO approved 108 ADFFs (for $96,300). Help was given for many different activities related to building local organizations. ADFF grants helped with specific technical training in areas such as nutrition, exchange of practical experiences among small groups of farmers and promoters, evaluations of the socioeconomic impact of local development agencies, and analysis of the feasibility of long-term projects. Limited funds as "seed money" were provided to start the implementation of specific development projects.

1983–87: EXPANDING COOPERATION

In 1983 a letter from the director of one of LWR's partner organizations said, "I thank you fraternally for your efficient help in carrying out the project in reference [a project entitled "Highland Peasant Training and Promotion"]. I believe that we are at the culmination of a phase in which PEBAL has learned much from LWR....I hope that from now on our joint work will be carried on in the same fraternal spirit and with the best of results."[9]

The work was so encouraging that LWR began to increase its support of local NGO development work. An open attitude and interest in experimenting with new alternatives for development, aided by increased availability of resources during this period, made it possible to augment considerably its involvement in longer-term projects as well as continuing a steady number of small grants (ADFFs).

During this five-year period, ARO gave $127,000 through 109 small projects (ADFFs). These micro-grants were able to cover a wide range of activities that would have been difficult to support through a conventional method of international cooperation. The funding of ADFFs "continued being a humble but important contribution in terms of assistance for groups which are critically examining their present development work. Experience confirms that...relatively insignificant amounts of finance can certainly make an impact on development activities way beyond the initial amount of investment."[10]

Learning continued to be a central activity for ARO through the small projects in both cities and rural areas. In these marginal areas the absence of government services was very noticeable, but it was also here where many NGOs and grassroots organizations demonstrated creativity and hard work in community-based efforts. Obviously these efforts, because they arose from the grassroots, were more appropriate for their environment and their own potential than externally planned proposals.

Also in 1983, to counterattack the effects of the Niño Current, which caused floods in the north of Peru and a prolonged drought in the south, LWR used "emergency help" in order to aid the communities affected by these natural disasters. This was repeated after the floods in 1985, when Lake Titicaca in the south of Peru overflowed its banks. Though these efforts were initially relief response, various opportunities grew out of these emergency programs for long-term development with grassroots organizations.

Resources invested in training continued to upgrade NGO personnel and increase their understanding of development projects as processes. ARO continued to facilitate events that made learning possible. Several small books were published with the aim of "socializing" information, that is, sharing what had been done. Subjects included social action, management, evaluation, the church and social action, and institutional crisis management.

LIMITATIONS AND DIFFICULTIES

The work was not without difficulties. The strategy of supporting a large number of small and diverse projects in many different parts of the country and the increased number of longer-term projects made it more and more difficult for the ARO team to maintain adequate contact with the projects being financed. In this respect a 1987 study reported that "several people who were interviewed complained... that since the number of projects supported by LWR had increased in the region, accompaniment had lost its momentum and its quality tended to decline once the donations had been approved."[11]

So even though it was possible to increase LWR's level of assistance, it was important to define the extent of ARO's presence and work in the region. The 1987 evaluation suggested that "LWR should more precisely formulate its long-range objectives and plans for its development as an institution."[12]

1988–90: CONCENTRATING COOPERATION

ARO proceeded to work internally in response to a series of weaknesses that were identified by the 1987 evaluations. A series of meetings with the NGO counterparts began. In a letter to ARO's partners, the new director wrote,

> We are in the process of implementing changes.... Since the stated recommendations have come basically from you, we would like to ask you to help us so that we can plan our work for 1988 together. We would also like to bring you up to date regarding the present situation of LWR/ARO with respect to how our office is going to function and the situation of our budget, so that together we can decide the type of accompaniment to be given to the centers (NGOs) and to the program as a whole.[13]

A "Global Strategy for the Andean Region" (1988–92) was prepared as well as a strategy for each of the countries of the region. This was based principally on an analysis of the sociopolitical situation and defined priorities more precisely by programmatic area and objectives and plans for the programs in each country.

In response to a strong interest from partners, ARO published a manual for self-evaluation of development projects. This manual put special emphasis on helping local teams design their own evaluations. In a letter to partner organizations the ARO director wrote, "Having completed ten years of presence in the Andean Region, LWR wants to offer this evaluation tool with the desire of contributing from our years of experience to the accompaniment of local NGOs in their efforts to do better work through reflection and evaluation."[14]

ARO also published a book entitled *Women and Popular Sectors: Issues and Alternatives* in order to facilitate a better understanding of women's roles in their search for solutions to their daily problems, "stimulating deep reflection within the different churches regarding what they can do to change the present situation of women."[15]

During this period of consolidation and shrinking budgets, small grants decreased and the portfolio of NGO projects supported by LWR in the Andean region dropped from thirty-three to twenty-one by 1989.

The new strategy called for some changes:

> ARO will have an increasing interest in putting into practice the concept of "agglutination," which means concentrating the activities within districts or geographical regions in each country in order to facilitate a more intense accompaniment and create an accumulative effect in development activities. In this way, exchange among different projects and communities...will promote their reproduction in neighboring areas.[16]

1979–89: TEN YEARS OF ACCOMPANIMENT

During its first ten years of work, LWR/ARO progressively became more conscious of the complexity and interrelatedness of social problems. ARO's various experiences have added to a more complete understanding of its role in the development process. In a ten-year period, LWR invested $3,113,256 in Peru, obviously a small amount in the face of such overwhelming needs. Of this amount, approximately 70 percent had been designated for the rural sector. The challenge has been to work against the marginalization of Andean *campesinos,* and to support their valiant attempts at freeing themselves from the prison of poverty to which five hundred years injustice have condemned them.

Nevertheless, the fact that even in their poverty the *campesinos* find mechanisms for eluding the pressures of the dominant social system is encouraging. We respect them for their efforts, for their cultural richness, and for the value of their knowledge. In this we see signs of hope. It is also a recognition that the work done by local NGOs is important and is contributing to the development process, so the "country bumpkins," as one of our colleagues in Peru[17] calls them, can fulfill their own destiny as human beings.

Chapter Eleven

TOGETHER AS PARTNERS

The purpose for the existence of most church-related relief and development agencies has to do with showing love to the neighbor in need.

For example, Lutheran World Relief's policy states that "the program of LWR is an expression of Christian love, conveyed through actions which respond to human need through the lives of those who work with the poor."[1] Many other international humanitarian relief and development agencies express their purpose in similar terms. Agencies such as these exist to serve their less fortunate neighbors.

One of the most poignant teachings on acting in love toward one's neighbor is found in Luke 10 and can be seen as a fundamental motivation for this principle. This parable of the Good Samaritan is told in response to a lawyer who engages Jesus in a polemic on the law and salvation. To Jesus' question about how he understood the law of Moses, the lawyer replied that we are to love our neighbors as ourselves. But the lawyer wanted to debate the question "Who is my neighbor?" probably in an attempt to justify his own shortcomings in loving his own neighbors. He would rather split hairs then act on what Jesus was pointing to — helping anyone in need.

The Samaritan showed compassion (love), and the lawyer recognized that the Samaritan had shown mercy and was the real neighbor. Without the final passage of the parable, however, the impact of this teaching would be lost. "Go and do likewise" connects belief, statement of purpose, and commitment to action. This is what is meant by the attempt to act as a Good Samaritan and help the one found beaten along the roadside.

ACTING IN SOLIDARITY

"Solidarity" is a somewhat overused term, but it is a concept that has meaning only when acted out in real life. Solidarity means sensitivity and commitment to the struggles, pains, and fears of people living in conditions of poverty and oppression. It implies a readiness to respond appropriately and in a timely manner to the varied needs that arise. When needs are real and concrete, our reactions must be concrete as well.

O'Gorman says that when human promotion (i.e., work with the poor) is centered on "doing for" and not on "commitment with," it is difficult to attack the roots of the real problems.[2]

When the offices of one the NGOs that LWR supports in Peru were bombed, the team was in shock. They had gone through a terrifying experience and needed help. So they came to Pedro (LWR's staff person) to talk, to be listened to, to sort out feelings and fears, and to start to put together plans to recuperate themselves as individuals and as an organization. Pedro did not and could not offer to solve their problems with money. Rather, he spent time with the team and listened to them with his heart. He brought wisdom and concern to the many meetings and visits with the team over a period of several months.

"In the same way, faith by itself, if it is not accompanied by action, is dead" (James 2:14–17). Reading these words we might naturally picture a "have" and a "have-not," a rich person and a poor person. We envision a one-way flow of resources, at least if the rich person will heed the words of James. But we might imagine another kind of exchange as well. The exchange is mutual as poor people combine their resources of spirit and organization.[3]

"Solidarity" is not just a catchy word used among brothers and sisters; rather it is being there when you are needed. It means presence for the other in response to real needs and pain, and it also means respect and equality in the relationship.

MUTUALITY

A relationship of partners implies give and take. It is a relationship of openness to dialogue and the exchange of points of view. Respect is of utmost importance. In one program I knew of in the Andean region, the local community actually decided to turn down a program being offered by an international agency. The agency raises funds through child sponsorships, and the community felt that too many requirements were attached to the receipt of the resources being offered.

Larry Minear points out that the giving of aid involves power for the agencies that provide it. "Over the years, in fact, aid has given agencies in the richer countries such power that groups on the receiving end are beginning to insist on more mutuality.... Greater mutuality is likely to mean reduced power for what used to be called 'donor agencies' and more accountability to those receiving aid."[4]

One of the objectives of accompaniment is to generate conditions of mutual respect and confidence to create an atmosphere of fraternal understanding as well as criticism. An indicator of whether or not we are achieving this objective is how our role is perceived by our partners in the Andean region in relation to the churches in the United States. LWR's partners have often asked us to find ways to communicate project experiences as well as the social, political, and economic realities of Latin America to our churches in the North. They see our relationship as one in which they can participate and give much to us, not only one in which we are the "donors" and they the "recipients."

Bishop Leónidas Proaño of Ecuador talked about respect in relationship with the people:

> I speak of a respectful accompaniment, one that does not trample.... We have to be very careful not to fall into what the people express as thinking for them and doing for them; if we think for them and if we do for them, we will never reach the point where the *campesinos* can be the protagonists of their own history, where they can be the main actors, the makers of their own development as was discussed in the Medellín conference.[5]

Proaño practiced an accompaniment of mutual respect, friendship, and love, which led to trust.

TRUST

Trust is an obvious value for any working relationship and clearly very important in a partnership that crosses many boundaries. The relationship of an international church-related agency with a national partner is at least four-pronged: international, interinstitutional, interpersonal, and cross-cultural, all at the same time. In such a relationship we are open to the risks of misunderstanding, and there is the need for clearly expressed interests and aspirations on both sides. Transparency in what we each want and intend is the basis for honest relationships between partners.

The relationship that involves the transfer of resources requires hard-headed business principles, such as reporting, accountability, and good stewardship. However, in the final analysis, we have to depend on a trusting relationship rather than legal conditions and threats. This may be one of the principal differences between private assistance programs and government-to-government programs.

An indicator for measuring the level of confidence we

are developing with an NGO, and therefore the possibility of helping them with their needs, is the facility with which it is possible to dialogue with the leaders of the institution, the team, and community leaders. In the Andean region we have received many requests for help with problems and very few cases of covering up problems, fraud, or the misuse of resources in the years of working with our partners.

ACCOUNTABILITY

Within cooperative relationships, there are both rights and obligations. One of the most important of the obligations is that of fiscal responsibility and reporting, and it is on this point where there is much debate about partnership. Can we talk about partnership when one partner has the money and the other has to ask for it? One partner has the power to decide who get funds and how much and the other is accountable for their use? There is no fully satisfactory answer to this dilemma. That fact, however, does not make partnership a less desirable ideal. It is an ideal worthy of much effort.

BUILDING PARTNERSHIP

The word "accompaniment," as we have said, has been used by the team of Lutheran World Relief in the Andean region to try to explain a working relationship between partners. I refer here to the partnership between the international agency and the local NGO. The values discussed above need to be worked out in practical terms.

Those who have had the privilege to work in programs based on the principles of partnership have experienced unique relationships. This arises from the fact that one of the primary objectives of partnership is an interest in enhancing the potential of each partner to more efficiently use the resources of both to meet the needs of the poor. This allows us take a shortcut in getting to know what the problems are.

Specifically, what does each partner bring to the relationship? LWR provides funds, ideas, experience in development programs, and an interest in jointly working on solutions. The local partner brings human resources, knowledge of the national context, leverage with the local government, and contacts to draw upon for local resources. Together they can pool a wide array of information and resources.

Playing down the funding relationship with an NGO when beginning a new partnership and showing interest in learning about specific issues have made it possible to "stretch" the dialogue to such a point that we can really get to know each other. A small amount of support at critical points can do wonders for building the relationship and the capacity of partner NGOs.

We know from experience that one of these critical times in the life of a development project is in the beginning when a local NGO is building relationships with the communities. In this beginning stage it is generally difficult to obtain resources from funding agencies. The pressure to get a project funded can lead the team to assumptions that do not necessarily correspond to the priorities of the community.

Both partners place great emphasis on the expectations of the people in the community. The NGO introduces LWR staff to the community, giving us the opportunity to explain who we are, why we are interested in helping, what our motives are, where our resources come from, and how this money is raised. This phase permits dialogue that avoids creating confusion in the community in which the local NGO is a funding institution. It also contributes to helping the community to establish more clearly the limits of the local NGO and makes it possible to answer any questions the people may have regarding LWR. Some of the questions that arise are: What is Lutheran World Relief? Who are Lutherans? Where do you get your funds? Do we have to be Lutherans in order to receive assistance? What is the difference between Lutherans and Catholics? What do we have to give for what we receive? What things do you fund? Through these encounters we have come to see that even when the relationship with the NGO has already been initiated, dialogue with the community makes it possible to increase the understanding of what LWR is and establish a relationship of greater confidence.

During the implementation of the project, when LWR staff do field visits, the NGO invites us to participate in the team's work sessions with the population. This allows us to continue the dialogue and share both the experiences of other places and information from publications and training events. This is how LWR has been able to facilitate exchange visits for technicians and grassroots leaders to other groups and projects in the same or a neighboring country in order to learn from others who are facing similar problems. In some cases it has allowed us to find topics of common interest and organize training sessions. One example of this was the seminar on management that was given for professional NGO staff and peasant leaders of grassroots organizations.

AN OUTSIDE OBSERVER'S PERSPECTIVE

We asked Richard Clinton, who has pursued an interest in development issues in Peru from a theoretical and policy perspective for nearly three decades, to take a close-up view of three local development efforts that LWR accompanies in Peru. Some of his comments are instructive with regard to both the risks and opportunities inherent in the accompaniment approach and are quoted here:

> A fine but significant line separates accompaniment from paternalism. The subtlety of this fragile boundary may be an even more formidable obstacle to the widespread adoption of an accompaniment model of development assistance than is the obsession with timely and quantifiable outcomes.

Close contact between funders and the (local) NGOs they are funding is an open invitation to interference in the implementation of particular projects by the funders and the emergence of a dependent relationship on the part of the local NGOs. The temptation to offer constructive advice (read "direction") or to prevent apparently doomed approaches from being employed (read "overrule") is well-nigh impossible to resist for donors anxious to maximize the impact of their funds. It requires extraordinary restraint to resist such temptations. This restraint, in turn, requires (1) respect for the NGOs' autonomy, (2) acceptance of the reality that mistakes are one of the most certain sources of human learning, and (3) understanding that the emergence of free-standing, self-critical, and innovative problem-solving capacities is not only conducive to development but is a large part of what development is all about.

Even when all this is grasped and fully appreciated in theory, it takes a special combination of personality traits to put it into practice. Sympathetic listening, engaged questioning, nondirective suggesting, and solidarity in the face of setbacks are the stuff of accompaniment. How many development agencies have either the time or the sensitive and committed staff demanded by this approach? With determined effort, perhaps enough sensitive and caring people could be recruited and properly trained for wider use of the accompaniment model. But this highlights the question of how many development agencies would want to adopt it? The sad reality of much that passes for development assistance suggests that the potential subscribers to the accompaniment approach would be few.

From all I observed on these site visits to LWR/ARO-sponsored projects on the Peruvian coast, I concur with Albert O. Hirschman's assessment after his much more extensive inspection in 1983 of grassroots development efforts funded by the Inter-American Foundation: "a minimum of paternalism and much inventiveness."

There simply can be no question that the grassroots development phenomenon responds to a multitude of human needs that too often go unmet and thus not only improves poor people's lives but does so in ways that enhance their capacity to make these improvements self-sustaining. In addition to its multiple services to the poor, however, the contributions that the grassroots development approach makes to the Peruvian middle class and to Peru's long and torturous march toward democracy are perhaps equally important.[6]

STAYING POWER

The constant *presence* of LWR in a small region and continuous contact with project teams and local issues is one of the characteristics of accompaniment that helps consolidate relationships with partners. Comparing those places where LWR first began work with the places where the largest number of poor people are concentrated in Peru, it can be concluded that the choices were good. This concentration of projects has been maintained for more then a decade, facilitating an understanding of the context and the main problems of these localities. It has also taught us what type of help other funding agencies give.

Another characteristic of accompaniment that has contributed to program impact has been consistency of support, in other words, "stick-to-it-iveness." Although not always possible, not setting time limits on funding permits the NGO to be at least partially free from financial worry and to more responsibly assume its support for development in the medium term.

The projects presently funded by LWR are a response to the initiatives of poor people from the region. They are based on the conviction that, even with their scarce resources, the poor possess the necessary talent and aptitude for organizing to solve their own problems. In the beginning these were all new projects with no other sources of funding, and the first funding period was for two years. Usually the support was renewed for three years or more. ARO now has some partnerships with local organizations that span nine or ten years. ARO's presence and modest funding has, in many cases, helped the local organization to build up a capacity and show results, thus attracting funding from other sources. In the work of human development a short-term vision is not adequate for long-term problems and needs.

Chapter Twelve

INTO THE FUTURE
The Challenges of Accompaniment

In the preceding chapters I have described some experiences of helping the poor that private organizations have practiced in the Two-Thirds World. I have argued for an approach of accompaniment and partnership. Even as I write these concluding comments, I feel a sense of urgency about the challenges of development and transformation, not so much to communicate my ideas or urge others to accept them as a wish for a deeper and more intense dialogue that might lead to collective action on creative alternatives. This urgency is well expressed by David Korten:

> We have no more than an instant of historical time to accomplish a transformation in our values and institutions if we are to save ourselves and our host (our world) from the violence to one another and to nature caused by our short-sightedness.[1]

In these descriptions of experience and theory, I have used some terms that may seem a bit too much like professional jargon. I apologize if they get in the way of communicating what I feel are some of key ideas about accompanying the poor. As I review these terms, I find that there were four of them that seem to summarize what is essential to a theory and practice of accompaniment. All of

them start with the letter "p," and each has been exam-
ined in the foregoing text: *partnership, process, participation,*
and *priorities* — all aimed at people-centered development.

Alfred North Whitehead said "it takes a very unusual
mind to make an analysis of the obvious." The terrible state
of our world and the seemingly logical principles of accompaniment as an approach to the work of development and
transformation, in fact, do require very unusual people with
long-term dedication and vision.

DOING IT WITH VISION

He saw the trees before they appeared, the sun before
it rose, and dared to bring the future into the present.
— Rev. G. P. Sheriden, in a eulogy to Dr. Will Mayo, 1939

Now, let's get down to the nitty gritty.
— Sam Jacobson, chainsaw repairman, Kenyon, Minn., 1991

The above quotations illustrate two levels of eloquence as
well as two levels of involvement and thinking about human
endeavors. If applied to the concept of human development,
both visionaries and "hands-on" people are needed. Most
nongovernmental organizations, church-related and secular,
that work for equitable, sustainable and just development in
the world today have and need both types of people. The
visionary, Dr. Mayo, used both his mind and his hands in
his pioneering work in medicine. So also Sam, the hands-
on chainsaw mechanic, needs to use his mind as well as his
hands in his work. Both grassroots volunteers and executives
of churches and NGOs also need that balance.

The private and voluntary sector offers an alternative to
macro-level attempts by governments and large donors to
confront the problems of poverty and injustice. With rich
and diverse experience in the work of relief and development, NGOs have excellent potential as creative agents
for both the day-to-day grassroots work and the forging of
a vision for a transformed world. That vision must lead

large numbers of our populations to think globally and act locally. It must start with ourselves and the institutions in which we participate and which we support. Church-related agencies are particularly well positioned to challenge their denominations and supporters to participate in this task.

Individuals, as well as institutions, need to develop and articulate a vision of what a just and sustainable world would look like. If you are reading this book, in all like-lihood you can exercise power and can make decisions to practice stewardship over certain resources to a much greater degree than can most poor people. Power and the empowerment of the poor are bottom-line issues.

APPROPRIATE ROLES AND CHALLENGES

In our discussion of the accompaniment approach to helping the poor in the Andean region we said that while funding of projects is important, it is not the only nor necessarily the most important element of partnership. Other important roles are often mentioned, such as sharing of information, communication, education, research, advocacy, and policy analysis.

We tried not to make funding the center of our relationship. Yet it was my experience during four years as the director of the Andean Regional Office of Lutheran World Relief that local NGOs in each of the countries in which we worked were constantly searching for funds and were frequently running projects with "soft money," i.e., short-term budgets. Local leaders and administrators were often very concerned about "the next funding period" and needed to juggle budgets to keep projects going while funding agencies went through their sometimes laborious processing and decision-making procedures. Finding the resources for administration, planning, and pilot projects was even more difficult. Thus, partnership was never a completely clean-cut relationship divorced from the complexities of funding. The reality is that money and decisions about the use of it are ever present in our North-South relationships.

One of the most difficult features of this relationship of partners, however, comes into play when we take seriously the idea of empowerment of people. Supporting the process of empowerment means changing the perceptions of constituents and donors. It leads inevitably to political considerations. Certainly it is easier to raise funds for child sponsorships or relief programs than it is for a much more complicated notion of transformation and empowerment. As Charles Elliott has said, "Empowerment is not something that can be delivered or bought. It cannot be reduced to a project. It is a process. It is a process that depends more on people than highly trained experts, either local or expatriate.... This approach thus offers a very marginal role to the northern agencies."[2]

If empowerment and transformation are seen as an important agenda for the future, it is imperative for churches and NGOs in the North to creatively think through new roles and relationships. The challenge to accompany the poor and work for transformation is carried out at various levels: (1) the donors and church constituency, (2) the partner indigenous NGO, (3) the international NGO's field staff, and (4) headquarters staff and boards of directors.

PARTICIPATION BY PEOPLE IN THE PEW

With respect to the participation of people committed to the goal of human transformation, we might visualize a kind of three-tiered scheme. The majority at the base of this pyramid are the 90–95 percent who write a check or put money in the collection plate and leave it at that. It is, of course, essential to have a large number of informed supporters at the grassroots in northern countries that provide the resources to private organizations. The greater the understanding on the part of this majority of donors of the real needs of the poor and the critical condition of our world, the stronger will be the base for the transformation of our institutions and political and economic structures.

Though change and transformation require more than cursory review of fund-raising brochures and short video presentations, we have to recognize that the majority of people will participate at this contributor level, and their financial support is, of course, crucial and much appreciated. In my view, fund raisers should neither err on the side of presenting simplistic solutions to poverty and injustice nor on the side of expecting the majority of their donors to get deeply involved in complex issues of transformation. Raising funds should go hand in hand with raising consciousness.

The need for a cadre of volunteers, the 3 or 4 percent who live out their commitment by investing time and creative energy in a variety of activities, will be even more crucial in the future than it has been in the past. These volunteers come from the minority in any community or church who do most of the work and for whom the word "commitment" means acting on what they believe in the "nitty gritty" of everyday work.

Volunteers can do many things. They get involved in local committees to plan and organize fund-raising and educational events, network with solidarity groups, sponsor visitors from the Two-Thirds World, write letters to the editors of the local papers, form study groups, lead Sunday school forums on hunger and justice issues, and speak to service organizations and churches. Understanding issues and working for transformation in the future will require even more education and engagement with issues and people of other cultures and nations. There will be an increased need to "train for transformation." Church and NGO leadership need to work with congregations and communities to plan and carry out creative projects for training. One of the crucial elements is to build in support systems for volunteers that take into consideration the well-known risk of burn out.

The following quotation is from an excellent resource for training for transformation developed in Africa, though also useful for people at the grassroots in northern countries: "Transformation is at the heart of Christian revelation; a deep faith — as we read our newspaper — as we look around at the pain and suffering in the world — that the way things are now, is not the only way they can be."[3]

One of the most effective forms of training for transformation is the study tour to low-income countries to learn about the reality of poverty and injustice. The well-planned and well-executed study tour is an excellent educational opportunity that not only gives participants the chance to see and understand the work of development at the grassroots, but also provides exposure to poverty and injustice. There is no substitute for face-to-face encounters with people who are struggling for survival at the margins of society. Here is where it is possible to begin to understand the connection between poverty and its causes.

Often the initial reaction of a person who encounters the complexities of poverty and injustice is confusion and guilt. This is especially so when people begin to see a connection between our way of life and the poverty conditions of such large numbers of people in the countries being visited. The next important step is to find ways to empower people to move beyond guilt and confusion to work for change and transformation.[4]

THE ROLE OF THE NGO IN THE FIELD

The tiny minority who enter into the world of service and become involved full time with organizations and movements that work with the poor constitutes the third of the three tiers. As I have pointed out, it is unlikely that international NGO personnel will find their primary role in accompaniment at the grassroots in the Two-Thirds World as volunteers, advisors, or technical assistants to southern partners. Nevertheless, with regard to the placement of field offices and staff there is a need for a small number of capable and highly motivated people who are ready to make a long-term commitment to the poor and willing to live in and become totally immersed in countries and regions of the Two-Thirds World. Cross-cultural skills and an understanding of the socioeconomic and political realities of the country or region will be as important or more important than technical skills, though a balance of both is necessary. The role of information analysis and interpretation will be essential as these representatives of international NGOs attempt to make linkages between political, economic, and environmental concerns of both the North and South. Elliott has observed that "it seems that northern NGOs that have their own nationals in the field learn faster and more thoroughly than those who have withdrawn all expatriate staff and/or have a purely funding relationship with local NGOs."[5]

My feeling is that it is quite difficult for national staff of partner organizations to interpret and package information for use in the North. There are great benefits to maintaining a people-to-people connection through a minimal presence of expatriate personnel working with local staff in NGO field offices. Writing, interpretation, and education should be a major role and function of these representatives of international agencies and churches. Also, the capacity to accompany indigenous NGOs through planning, reflection, and evaluation will continue to be the nuts and bolts of their ongoing work, the nitty gritty, if you will.

The day-to-day administrative and accompaniment relationships with indigenous NGOs should be primarily in the hands of local people on the staff of the international NGO. Efforts should be made to form interagency teams from several like-minded international NGOs who would be supported by one administrative structure and to develop common criteria for the use of pooled resources from several agencies. Work with partner organizations that receive funding from several international donors could thus be better coordinated and accompanied. Teams would be formed of both expatriates (read North Americans or Europeans) as well as nationals from the country and region.

Decisions on the allocation of resources could be delegated to the field, especially for small projects, by forming screening committees constituted of representatives from both indigenous and international NGOs. Accountability and reporting on the use of funds is vital, and the international NGO community needs to do much homework on acceptable reporting standards so as to not create undue burdens and confusion in the partner NGOs. Also, much needs to be done to make progress reports and evaluations more interesting and useful for all concerned.

AT HEADQUARTERS

The trend toward greater professionalization of headquarters staff of NGOs will continue, probably with increased efforts to evaluate what these international organizations have accomplished during the last decades of involvement in development programs. These learnings should be applied in an attempt to forge a vision for the future based on the unique strengths and accomplishments of their own organization. Ideally, some of these staff should spend more of their time reflecting, documenting, and writing about the process of development and transformation and less on administrative details. That is not likely to happen unless the directors and boards of the institutions deliberately encourage it and structure their organizations to make it happen. This could mean experimenting with new forms of funding and project management and moving some of the decision making on fund allocation to field staff and/or partner NGOs in the South (as already mentioned).

Feedback from the field is crucial for institutional learning, constituency education, and advocacy. The theory that the international NGO can speak with authority on public policy and carry out its advocacy work because it has been informed by direct involvement and program activities in the field has not been strongly backed by practice, in my experience. Too often field staff of the international agency, whether expatriate or local, feel like they are out there in their country of assignment all alone like arms and legs disconnected from the head and body of the organization. Much more could be done to strengthen the linkage between what happens in the projects and the organization's work in education and advocacy at home.

CONCLUSIONS

So let us not become tired of doing good; for if we do not give up, the time will come when we will reap the harvest.

—Galatians 6:9

Herein may lie the main points of this book — doing good and reaping the harvest. Doing good means giving bread to the hungry, but it also means doing the work of justice and transformation. Reaping the harvest can be interpreted in both individualistic and global terms. We can continue on a course of unrestrained consumption for personal gratification or choose a course of service and stewardship toward a sustainable and equitable world. Setting priorities and making these choices confronts us all, and the time for doing so is upon us.

We share both individual and collective responsibilities for our world and its people. We individually decide how to use our resources of time, money, and ideas for the good of ourselves and others, just as the institutions in which we participate do.

The founder of Heifer Project International, Dan West, wrote from Spain in December 1937: "History has been alive since then for me [referring to his college days], but now I care more and more to help make it."[6] Dan West was one of the visionaries who has made a mark on history. Each of us, whether visionary or grassroots volunteer, can add our own marks to the working out of God's reign of justice as we continue to remember the poor.

Appendix

GROUP DISCUSSION QUESTIONS

One of the purposes of this book is to raise consciousness in North America about hunger and poverty and how church-related agencies respond to these needs. In order for us as individuals to make an impact, we all need the help and support of others. Individualism is not congruent with partnership and solidarity.

Working within a group or organization adds to a corporate sense of responsibility and accomplishment. Studying and discussing issues and questions is a good way to start. It is also an excellent way to continue to build solidarity with the poor through concrete actions.

Part II of this book lends itself most readily to group study and reflection. The following are a series of questions relating to each chapter in Part II. These questions can be used as discussion starters for a single session on "approaches to helping the poor." A series of sessions — perhaps four or five — could examine both attitudes and methods involved in the various approaches presented in the book.

Chapter Four:
The Assistance Approach to Helping the Poor

1. What do you think about giving direct assistance? Is the giving of direct assistance to destitute people enough of a response in and of itself?

2. If not, what more is needed?

141

3. When is it appropriate to give direct assistance (relief)? When is it not appropriate?

4. If you were the director of an agency whose purpose it is to help the poor and oppressed, how much priority would you give to the direct assistance approach?

5. How does it make you feel to give material, financial, or personal aid to the poorest of the poor?

6. Is nonpolitical humanitarian assistance possible?

7. Is it helpful to speak of spiritual poverty in contrast to material poverty?

Chapter Five:
The Teaching Approach to Helping the Poor

1. Some people think that education is the basic solution to all problems. What do you think?

2. When is teaching an appropriate method for helping the poor?

3. When, if ever, is it not appropriate?

4. What did your education experience teach you about poverty? What do schools teach children and youth about the conditions of poverty in the world today?

Chapter Six:
On Participatory Development

1. What examples have you seen in your own community of cooperation and participation for the common good? What are some of the obstacles?

2. What do you think about the basic assumptions of the participatory approach to human promotion, namely, that people will work in solidarity and good will for the good of the community?

3. When is the participatory approach appropriate and when is it not?

4. Do the agencies you know of and support espouse the participatory approach to helping the poor? What do they claim as the most important element in their approach to effectively help the poor?

Chapter Seven:
Beyond Development to Transformation

1. What do you think of the quotation by Martin Luther King found in this chapter (see p. 80)? What is required of us to be Good Samaritans and faithful to Christ's teaching in the parable (Luke 10:25–37)?

2. What programs do you know of that follow the criteria suggested at the end of this chapter (p. 87)? Can you think of other criteria that are important for transformational human promotion?

3. What attitudes and behaviors do you see in yourself that need to be transformed? In your church? Community? Country?

4. If you were the director of a church-related relief and development agency, how would you use the resources at your disposal to help the poor? What mixture of assistance, education, development, and transformation programs would you employ?

NOTES

Introduction

1. In 1976 one of the priests, William Woods, died when shot down in his plane. Subsequently people began to disappear. By the early 1980s many kidnappings were taking place, education and health workers being the prime targets. In 1982 the army launched Victory 82, and hundreds of cooperative members were massacred. From *Nosotros conocemos nuestra historia*, Iglesia Guatemalteca en Exilio, 1985.

Part 1: Wanderings through the Helping Profession

1. For a good historical review of the roots and growth of the U.S. Private Voluntary Organization sector, see John G. Sommer, *Beyond Charity: U.S. Voluntary Aid for a Changing Third World* (Washington, D.C.: Overseas Development Council, 1977).

2. Glee Yoder, *Passing On the Gift: The Story of Dan West* (Elgin, Ill.: Brethren Press, 1978).

3. Brian H. Smith, "Nonprofit Organizations and Socioeconomic Development in Colombia," ISPS Working Paper No. 2093 (Institute for Social and Policy Studies, Yale University, 1985). In his research in Colombia, Smith analyzed the work of local NGOs using several criteria: their ability to reach the poorest 40 percent and generate adequate new resources in the local environment to make them self-reliant; their empowerment of the poor to push from below for greater distribution of power; their role as catalysts to improve public policies toward the poor.

4. David C. Korten, "Micro Policy Reform: The Role of Private Voluntary Development Agencies," working paper (Washington, D.C.: National Association of Public Affairs and Administration, 1986).

5. For a succinct description of this concept in its more mature form see David C. Korten, "From Relief to People's Movement," in *Getting to the 21st Century: Voluntary Action and the Global Agenda* (West Hartford, Conn.: Kumarian Press, 1990), chap. 10, 113–32.

Chapter 1: Vietnam: Starting on the Cutting Edge

1. Several books were written that give insights into the experience from a personal perspective. See Mary Sue H. Rosenberger, *Harmless as Doves: Witnessing for Peace in Vietnam* (Elgin, Ill.: Brethren Press, 1988), and Earl Martin, *Reaching the Other Side* (New York: Crown Publishers, 1978).

2. Earl Martin, "Reflections on Our Vietnam Experience: Ten Years Later," *Missionary Messenger*, May 1985.

3. Lance R. Woodruff, "The Importance of Helping People," *Lutheran Women* 5 (May 1967).

Chapter 2: Peru: Learning at the Grassroots

1. David Archer and Patrick Costello, "Bolivia, El Alto: The Language of Power" in *Literacy and Power: The Latin America Battleground* (London: Earthscan Publications, 1990), 171.

2. For a fascinating account of travels through the world's last great wilderness, the Amazon, see Jonathan Kandell, *Passage through El Dorado* (New York: Avon Books, 1984).

3. From a conversation with Terry Gips, president of the International Alliance for Sustainable Agriculture, 1701 University Avenue S.E., Minneapolis, Minn., July 1992.

Chapter 3: Nicaragua: The Right Place at the Right Time

1. The term "Latin America" generally refers to all the "Latin" countries lying south of the U.S. Central America is the region encompassing the countries south of Mexico — Guatemala, Honduras, El Salvador, Nicaragua, and Costa Rica. Panama is also considered a part of Central America, though it does form a sort of bridge between Central and South America.

2. From "CEPAD's Development Philosophy and Models: The First 15 Years," November 1988: "CEPAD is a Nicaraguan church-based organization with a five million dollar budget and 24 offices throughout the country. It has some 220 paid staff and literally thousands of volunteers active in various programs. . . . In 1987 it is actively providing development services in 203 communities and indirectly affecting the development in 200 others."

3. CEPAD Annual Report, 1973, 3.

4. Ibid.

5. Jerry Aaker, "Training Leaders for Development: Reflections on a Latin American Experience," unpublished paper, 1976.

6. Section 2.6 of the 1987–89 CEPAD Program Plan.

Part 2: Promoting Human Dignity

1. *A Generation in Crisis: Boys and Girls in Latin America and the Caribbean* (New York: National Council of the Churches of Christ in the U.S.A., 1990).

2. Wayne G. Bragg, "From Development to Transformation," in *The Church in Response to Human Need*, edited by Vinay Samuel and Chris Sugden (Grand Rapids: Wm. B. Eerdmans Publishing Company, 1987). The four models described by Bragg are modernization theory, dependency theory, global reformism, and another development. His study includes a critique of each and concludes that none of them offers a theory complete enough to bring about real change and lasting solutions.

3. John P. Lewis, "Strengthening the Poor: Some Lessons for the International Community," in *Strengthening the Poor: What Have We Learned?* (New Brunswick, N.J.: Transaction Books, 1988), 6. Lewis cites several central texts as giving guidance to this reform agenda, including the World Bank's *Redistribution with Growth* (1974), and the ILO'S *Employment, Growth and Basic Needs* (1976). Subsequently, USAID followed this line of thinking and adopted the "new directions" that contained most of these same reforms.

4. Frances O'Gorman and the CEAR team, *Promoción humana (dignificación)* (San José, Costa Rica: World Vision, 1990).

Chapter 4: How Do We Spell Relief?

1. From *Human Development Report 1990* (New York: United Nations Development Program, 1990).

2. LWR Annual Reports for the years 1986, 1987, and 1988 show that the total disbursements of the agency for those three years was $97,960,000, of which $72,409,000 was expended in the categories "Relief Services" and "Gifts in Kind Shipped." The majority of this assistance went to sub-Sahara Africa, which suffered severe famine during most of the 1980s. Thus, though LWR emphasizes the development side of its work, these figures show that 74 percent of LWR's resources went to relief during these three years. In 1990, a year of even more dramatic risk of widespread famine in Sudan and Ethiopia, LWR channeled a huge amount of food to try to avert mass starvation. The annual audit for that year showed that LWR's total expenditures were $93,461,000 and that almost 95 percent of that amount went to relief.

3. World Commission in Environment and Development, *Our Common Future* (Oxford: Oxford University Press, 1987).

4. Larry Minear, *Humanitarianism under Siege: A Critical Review of Operation Lifeline Sudan* (Trenton: Red Sea Press, 1991), 6. Church

World Service presents in this book an analysis of a major international response to the famine and civil war in Sudan in the late 1980s.

5. Jason W. Clay, "The West and the Ethiopian Famine: Implications for Humanitarian Assistance" (Cambridge, Mass.: Cultural Survival, 1986).

6. LWR issue paper "LWR Work in the Area of Conflict Resolution." This discussion paper recognizes that "sometimes supporting the poor and the oppressed means helping them to narrow the gap which exists between themselves and the rich. Empowering the poor can cause resistance among the non-poor."

7. From *Veja*, a Brazilian magazine, September 1979, as quoted by O'Gorman, *Promoción humana*, 22.

8. Ibid.

9. Jerry Aaker, "A Cup of Water," *Lutheran Standard*, March 18, 1983.

Chapter 5: Is Knowledge Enough?

1. "Balance Sheet of Human Development," *Human Development Report, 1990* (New York: United Nations Development Program, 1990), 27.

2. David Archer and Patrick Costello, *Literacy and Power: The Latin American Battleground* (London: Earthscan Publications, 1990), 101. This is an excellent compendium of case studies of innovative Latin American experiences with literacy and popular education.

3. *Promoción humana*, 36–37.

4. Archer and Costello, *Literacy and Power*, 19.

5. Ibid., "Appendix: The Life of Paulo Freire."

6. Leónidas E. Proaño, "Rural Organization in Central Ecuador," a presentation made at a round table discussion on the subject and published by FEPP (Fondo Ecuatoriano Populorum Progressio), Quito, 1989. The English translation was prepared by the Andean Regional Office of Lutheran World Relief.

7. National Consultation on Evangelization of the Evangelical Churches in Rio de Janeiro, 1980, *Tempo e Presença*, 11, quoted by O'Gorman, *Promoción humana*, 42.

Chapter 6: The Participation Principle

1. LWR Policy Statement, January 1, 1985.

2. This definition as well as the one for education above is attributed to Stephen Vetter in "Portrait of a Peasant Leader, Ramon Aybar," in *Direct to the Poor: Grassroots Development in Latin America*

(Boulder: Lynne Rienner Publishers, 1988). This is a book of case studies from projects supported by the Inter-American Foundation in Latin America. The book explores an approach to development used by IAF, which is based on the assumption that the "best way to help poor people is to give money to the organizations that they themselves create and control. IAF calls that approach "grassroots development," and is based on the belief that... poor people possess substantial resources, including knowledge and understanding of their circumstances,... and the capacity to organize and mount collective action" (from the introduction of the book).

3. LWR Policy Statement.

4. Karen L. Anderson, "A Time to Speak: Promoting Health in the Shantytown, *World Encounter* 2 (1989).

5. Patrick Breslin, *Development and Dignity* (Rosslyn, Va.: Inter-American Foundation, 1987).

6. Sheldon Annis and Peter Hakim, "What Is Grassroots Development?" in *Direct to the Poor: Grassroots Development in Latin America.*

Chapter 7: Relief, Development, and What Else?

1. See David C. Korten, *Getting to the 21st Century: Voluntary Action and the Global Agenda* (West Hartford, Conn.: Kumarian Press, 1990), 133.

2. James DeVries, "Development or Transformation? Reflections on a Holistic Approach to People-Centered Change." in *Heifer International Exchange* 63 (November/December 1991).

3. Ibid.

4. Vinay Samuel and Chris Sugden, eds. *The Church in Response to Human Need* (Grand Rapids: Wm. B. Eerdmans Publishing Company, 1987), 42.

5. A motto of the Sarvodaya Sharmadana movement in Sri Lanka.

6. Martin Luther King, Jr., *Beyond Vietnam and Casualties of the War in Vietnam* (New York: Clergy and Laity Concerned, 1985), 15.

7. O'Gorman, *Promoción humana*, 82, quoting newspaper articles in *Jornal do Brazil.*

8. United Nations, "State of the World's Women Report, 1985," prepared for the World Conference on the United Nations Decade for Women held in Nairobi, Kenya, 1985.

9. Earl S. Martin, "Reflections on Our Vietnam Experience: Ten Years Later," *Missionary Messenger*, May 1985.

10. LWR issue paper, "LWR Work in the Area of Conflict Resolution," June 1991.

11. Lester R. Brown and others, *State of the World, 1986: A Worldwatch Institute Report on Progress toward a Sustainable Society* (New York: W. W. Norton & Co., 1986), 199.

12. Larry Minear, "Humanitarian Aid in a World of Politics," *Lutheran Partners*, March/April 1989.

13. DeVries, "Development or Transformation?"

14. Several of these ideas come from David C. Korten, "NGO Self-Assessment Questions," in *Getting to the 21st Century*, 228–29.

Chapter 8: Some Often-Asked Questions

1. From an HPI brochure entitled, "Twenty Commonly Asked Questions and Answers about Heifer Project International."

2. See David M. Beckmann, Timothy J. Mitchell, and Linda L. Powers, *The Overseas List: Opportunities for Living and Working in Developing Countries* (Minneapolis: Augsburg Publishing House, 1985). This is a guide to organizations offering opportunities in foreign countries, written especially for Christians who are looking for ways to serve or study abroad.

3. Several church-related agencies that occasionally utilize personnel overseas are the following:

Catholic Relief Services, 209 West Fayette Street, Baltimore, MD 21201 (301-625-2220)

Church World Service, 475 Riverside Drive, New York, NY 10115 (212-870-2257)

Lutheran World Relief, 390 Park Avenue South, New York, NY 10016 (212-532-6350)

Heifer Project International, P.O. Box 808, Little Rock, AR 72203 (501-376-6836)

4. For more information contact the Mennonite Central Committee, 21 South 12th Street, P.O. Box 500, Akron, PA 17501-0050 (717-859-1151)

5. Several other organizations that may place volunteers overseas (or act as a clearinghouse) are the following:

American Friends Service Committee, 1501 Cherry Street, Philadelphia, PA 19102-1479 (215-241-7000)

Global Health Ministries Foundation, 122 West Franklin, Suite 600, Minneapolis, MN 55404

Lutheran World Mission Volunteer Program, Evangelical Lutheran Church in America, 8765 W. Higgins Road, Chicago, IL 60631

Habitat for Humanity, Habitat and Church Streets, Americus, GA 31709-3498 (912-924-6935)

Part 3: Toward a Practice of Accompaniment

1. Mario Padrón, "NGDOs and Grassroots Development in Latin America," 18th International Congress of Latin American Studies Association, Boston, 1986.
2. Ibid., 15.

Chapter 9: Latin America: The Context

1. Some of the ideas in this section are from a conversation with Jorge Alvarez Calderón, a Catholic priest who practices pastoral work in a slum area of Lima. Jorge is an associate of Gustavo Gutiérrez, considered to be one of the seminal thinkers of liberation theology. Both are associated with the Bartolomé de Las Casas Institute in Lima, Peru.
2. For a monumental documentation of the role of the "new Catholic Church" in Latin America and the resultant persecution and martyrdom of many who took this option, see Penny Lernoux, *Cry of the People* (New York: Doubleday & Company, 1980).
3. Melinda Roper, "Do This in Remembrance of Me: Discipleship in the Face of Evil," *Sojourners* (December 1990): 17–18.
4. Wayne G. Bragg, "From Development to Transformation," in Samuel and Sugden, eds. *The Church in Response to Human Need,* 29–31. Bragg gives a good review and critique of the dependency theory and lists six reasons why some of its assumptions are considered debatable.
5. Juan Sánchez, "An Agenda for North/South Cooperation: The Challenge to NGOs," November 1990. Sánchez, who works with a Peruvian NGO, made a presentation to the LWR Andean team in Lima in which he talked about the weakening of peasant organizations and unions in Peru and Bolivia in recent years in conjunction with the neoliberal economic adjustment policies that have been imposed in those countries.
6. Thomas W. Dichter, "The Changing World of Northern NGOs: Problems, Paradoxes, and Possibilities," in John P. Lewis et al., *Strengthening the Poor: What Have We Learned?* (New Brunswick, N.J.: Transaction Books, 1988), 183–84.

7. Mario Padrón, "NGDOs and Grass-Roots Development in Latin America," a paper presented to the 13th international congress of the Latin American Studies Association in Boston, October 1986. Mario Padrón worked with DESCO, a research center in Lima, and did pioneering thinking on the role and relationships between the northern and southern NGOs. He preferred to add the "D" for "development" to the acronym, i.e., NGDO.

Chapter 10: Accompaniment:
An Experiment in the Andean Region

1. LWR's primary support of relief and development activities in Latin America was directed to Brazil and Chile in the 1960s and 1970s.

2. An LWR staff person, J. Robert Busche, made an extensive survey in six Latin American countries in 1978 "to view at close range the activities, initiatives and relationships of a large number of development assistance agencies in the South." The impressions and conclusions arrived at as a result of this survey became the basis for attempting to forge a "new approach" to development, which was used when the Andean Regional Office was established the following year.

3. "Institutional Learning Process," LWR/ARO evaluation, May 1987.

4. The Latin American bishops' meeting in Medellín, Colombia, in 1968, is considered the event where the church deliberately made a change to take the side of the poor.

5. David Korten and Rudi Klauss, eds., *People-Centered Development* (West Hartford, Conn.: Kumarian Press, 1984). Korten argues that one critical distinction between production-centered and people-centered development is that the former routinely subordinates the needs of people to those of the production system, while the latter seeks consistently to subordinate the needs of the production system to those of people.

6. Patrick Breslin, *Development and Dignity* (Rosslyn, Va.: Inter-American Foundation, 1987).

7. Letter from Hans J. Hoyer to Center of Assistance of Rural Projects and Studies, CAPER, April 16, 1979.

8. Letter from Father John Hughes to LWR/ARO, March 18, 1981.

9. Letter to ARO from Edilberto Portugal, director of PEBAL (a Cusco-based NGO that LWR worked with), July 1983.

10. "Global Analysis of ADFFs," 1984.

11. Contribution to the LWR/ARO institutional reflection, GREDES, June 1987.

12. "The Process of Institutional Learning," LWR/ARO evaluation, May 1987.

13. Letter from ARO to its counterparts, December 2, 1987.

14. "A Process Approach to Self-Evaluation," LWR/ARO, 1989.

15. "Mujer y protagonismo popular en la región andina" (Women and leadership in the Andean region), published in March 1989.

16. LWR/ARO strategy statement, 1988–92.

17. Guido Delrán is the director of the Center for Andean Rural Studies "Bartolomé de las Casas," in Cusco, an institution that LWR has accompanied since 1981.

Chapter 11: Together as Partners

1. LWR Policy Statement, 1987.

2. Frances O'Gorman, *Promoción humana* (San José, Costa Rica: World Vision, 1990), 127.

3. Gerald W. Schlabach, *And Who Is My Neighbor? Poverty, Privilege, and the Gospel of Christ* (Scottdale, Pa.: Herald Press, 1990), 93.

4. Larry Minear, "Humanitarian Aid in a World of Politics," *Lutheran Partners*, March/April 1989.

5. Leónidas E. Proaño, "Rural Organization in Central Ecuador," a talk published by FEPP (Fondo Ecuatoriano Populorum Progressio), 1989.

6. Richard Clinton, "Grassroots Development Where No Grass Grows: Small-Scale Development Efforts on the Peruvian Coast," in *Studies in Comparative International Development*, Summer 1991.

Chapter 12: Into the Future: The Challenges of Accompaniment

1. David C. Korten, *Getting to the 21st Century: Voluntary Action and the Global Agenda* (West Hartford, Conn.: Kumarian Press, 1990), 214.

2. Charles Elliott, "Some Aspects of Relations between the North and South in the NGO Sector," in *World Development* 15 (1987): 59.

3. Anne Hope and Sally Timmel, *Training for Transformation: A Handbook for Community Workers* (Harare, Zimbabwe: Mambo Press, 1984). This is a series of three books with dozens of ideas and exercises in each to help facilitate self-reliant creative communities.

The books have as their basic philosophy the belief that we should all participate in making this world a more just place to live in.

4. The Center for Global Education, Augsburg College, 731 21st Avenue South, Minneapolis, MN 55454 (612-330-1159), is on the forefront of this kind of experiential education. It organizes travel seminars for diverse groups from all over the U.S. to many parts of the world. The center publishes a quarterly newsletter called *Global Perspectives.*

5. Elliott, "Some Aspects of Relations between the North and South in the NGO Sector," 58.

6. Glee Yoder, *Passing On the Gift: The Story of Dan West* (Elgin, Ill.: Brethren Press, 1978), 168.

INDEX

poverty,
 alleviating, 46–48
 biblical concept of, 3–7
 options for helping, 47–87
 statistics on, 45–46, 60
Proaño, Bishop Leónidas, 64,
  125
PROVADENIC, 62
public policy, U.S., 84–85
Pucallpa, Peru, 31–32

questions from sponsors, 88–98

Roper, Melinda, 106
Rother, Stan, 3
Rupel, Lucy West, 10

Sahara, 52
Ser con mi Hermano ("Being
  with my Brother"), 101–2
Smith, Brian H., 10–11
sponsors
 contacts with, 43–44
 participation of, 135–37
 questions of, 88–98
Studabaker, Ted, 16
study tour, 137

Thorp, David, 63–64
transformation
 agenda for, 87
 in development, 77–87

limitations of approach, 85–87
process of, 80–81
training for transformation,
  136–37
"Two-Thirds World," definition
  of, 6

UN World Summit on En-
  vironment (1992),
  30

Veliz, Pedro, 116
Vietnam, 13–22
 arrival in, 14
 letter from, 16–18
 Peace Witness in, 16–17
 reaction of people in, 20–21
Vietnam Christian Service
  (VNCS), 13–22, 83
 results of work of, 21
volunteer programs, 93–95
volunteers, 136–37
Voordeckers, Walter, 3

West, Dan, 10, 140
WILD (Women in Livestock
  Development), 81
withdrawal from projects, 36
women, in development, 81,
  96–98
Woods, Bill, 3